THE JUST BENTO
COOKBOOK

THE JUST BENTO COOKBOOK

Everyday Lunches To Go

Makiko Itoh

Photographs by Makiko Doi

KODANSHA USA

Published by Kodansha USA, Inc.
451 Park Avenue South
New York, NY 10016

Distributed in the United Kingdom and continental Europe
by Kodansha Europe Ltd.

ISBN 978-1-56836-393-6

First published in Japan in 2010 by Kodansha International
First US edition 2011 published by Kodansha USA

Printed in the United States of America.

18 17   9 8 7

The Library of Congress has cataloged the earlier printing as follows:

    Library of Congress Cataloging-in-Publication Data

Itoh, Makiko.
  The just bento cookbook : everyday lunches to go / Makiko Itoh ;
photographs by Makiko Doi.
     p. cm.
  Includes index.
  ISBN 978-4-7700-3124-2
  1. Cooking, Japanese. 2. Bento cooking. I. Doi, Makiko. II. Title.
  TX724.5.J3I85 2010
  641.5952--dc22
                        2010021074

www.kodanshausa.com

Contents

RECIPES: JAPANESE-STYLE BENTOS 13

RECIPES: NOT-SO-JAPANESE BENTOS 73

Introduction

A bento is a meal that is packed into a box. While in Japan there are several kinds of bentos, including large, elaborate presentation bentos served in restaurants, this book is about the compact, portable bento-box meals that anyone can make—the Japanese equivalent of a packed lunch.

Bento-box lunches were a part of my life growing up in Japan. My mother used to make bentos for my sisters and me to bring to school almost every day, as well as for family outings and picnics. One of my earliest food memories is of peering over the edge of a table, watching my aunts make dozens of onigiri rice balls for a big family gathering, their palms bright red from the salty, hot rice. I can still recall opening up my first bento box—a bright pink plastic one with matching chopsticks—on my first day at kindergarten; having my grilled salmon stolen out of my aluminum bento box in fifth grade by the boy sitting next to me; the great gabfests my friends and I had at lunchtime in high school as we swapped delicious morsels of food from our boxes.

After living most of my adult years in the United States and Europe, I turned back to bento lunches a few years ago. My aims were to use bento boxes to relearn portion control, to help with my weight-loss efforts, to eat healthier lunches, and to just get out of the fast-food rut I was in. Perhaps most of all, I wanted to reacquaint myself with this often creatively challenging way of presenting a variety of food in such a compact container.

In October 2007, I started a website called JustBento.com as a companion to my existing Japanese cooking site JustHungry.com, to share my renewed enthusiasm for bento-box meals with the world. The response from readers around the world, from all walks of life, has been overwhelming—from mothers who want to pack healthy lunches for their kids, students on a tight budget, people looking to lose weight or deal with food allergies in a creative way, to those who simply prefer delicious and economical homemade lunches to fast-food fare.

I've created more than 150 easy-to-prepare, original, bento-box–friendly recipes especially for this book. Some of the recipes are traditionally Japanese; some are inspired by other cuisines. With a little preplanning, all of the bentos in this book can be assembled in less than twenty minutes in the morning.

A bento-box lunch is really just a packed lunch—but it's a packed lunch prepared with a little extra care, for your family and loved ones, or just for yourself. Bento-box meals are satisfying to the eye and the soul, as well as the body. They do not have to be overly cute or take hours to prepare. With minimal effort and a splash of creativity, they can be things of simple beauty that not only bring a smile to the recipient's face but can be as pleasurable to make as they are to eat. I hope that this book will inspire you to make bento-box meals a regular part of your life.

Makiko's Top Ten Bento Rules

Make the bento healthy and balanced

I make sure to include protein and carbohydrates in every bento box. I always add vegetables, and often a little fruit too, but usually just for dessert, since fruit has a lot of sugar in addition to all those good vitamins. I prefer to get my vitamins and minerals, as well as fiber, from vegetables. Besides, vegetables are so colorful. In my bentos vegetables are not an afterthought—they take a starring role alongside the other main ingredients.

Since I'm usually watching my weight, I also try to keep the total calorie count down. With a few exceptions, all of the bentos in this book are around 600 calories or less. You can adjust this to fit your nutritional needs by packing more or less food in your bento box.

Keep the bento simple

I don't have the time to spend making multiple items for my bentos. I stick to a maximum of four or five different items per box; many of my bentos contain three items or less.

Make sure the bento is tasty

Any bento I make has to taste so good that the eater (whether it's me or someone else) looks forward to lunchtime all morning. I never, ever pack something just because it's supposed to be healthy. I also make sure that the food I put in tastes good even when cold or at room temperature, since that's how most bentos are eaten.

Make the bento, fun, colorful, and attractive, but don't fuss too much

We eat with our eyes as well as our mouths and stomachs. A bento box should look colorful and appetizing. I keep elaborate, time-consuming bento decoration attempts for special occasions, however. I have a general rule of keeping bento decorating time—the time needed for the addition of things like cutely cut vegetables—to a maximum of ten minutes per bento for everyday bentos. Usually it takes me no more than five minutes to add a fun, decorative element. You'll find a number of easy and quick bento decoration ideas throughout the book. Also keep in mind that a well-balanced, colorful bento can be beautiful on its own without any additional frills.

Use seasonal, locally grown, natural ingredients whenever possible

I try to make use of seasonal produce as much as possible. I also try to stay away from ready-made, processed foods. Most of my bentos are made with fresh, natural ingredients—organic and untreated fruits and vegetables, and ethically raised meat and poultry. When I do use processed foods, such as canned beans or processed meats, I try to stick to ones that have a minimum of additives. Sometimes I may stray from these rules for the sake of convenience, but I really do try to use them for all of my cooking, not just for bentos. Besides, in-season fruit and vegetables are usually cheaper and better tasting.

Pay attention to safety and hygiene

When packing food that may have to sit at room temperature for some time before being eaten, it's crucial to follow proper, safe, bento-packing practices. See Bento Safety Tips (page 12) for more details.

Plan ahead

The biggest time-waster in the morning is peering through the refrigerator and the cupboards, wondering what to make! I try to spend a few minutes every week planning out my bentos using my Weekly Meal Planner (page 117). I may not stick to the plan all the time, but it's so helpful to have some idea of what to pack beforehand.

Shop for bento-friendly foods

Shopping for groceries takes on a whole new dimension when you're planning to make bentos. Look especially for food that requires little or no cooking and fits nicely in a small box. Some things I buy regularly include very thinly sliced meats, bite-sized cheeses, single-serving packs of crackers, small bread rolls, tiny yogurt packs, and baby vegetables.

Keep costs down

Bringing a bento from home saves a lot of money over buying lunch from a fast-food place or eating out. To help me save even more money, I try to stick to economical cuts of meat and fish, and vegetables that are in season.

Don't try to replicate Japanese bentos made in Japan

I happen to love Japanese cuisine above all other cuisines—after all, I am Japanese! I don't try to replicate Japanese bentos that are made in Japan to the letter, however. While the increasing popularity of Japanese food worldwide has meant that staple ingredients such as soy sauce and miso are getting much easier to buy, many fresh ingredients that are taken for granted in Japan are hard or impossible to get outside of regions with large Japanese expatriate or immigrant populations. And even if you can get hold of them, they may be prohibitively expensive.

I live in a part of the world where the closest Japanese grocery store is too small to stock more than a few items of fresh produce. I believe that a lot of people reading this book may be in a similar predicament. For my everyday bentos, I make not only traditional, authentic-tasting, Japanese-style bentos that have been adapted to use ingredients that are widely available, but also bentos I have improvised over the years that combine various non-Japanese dishes and flavors.

I believe a homemade bento lunch is appealing because it is a healthy, attractive, and delicious meal, made with care and attention, that is compact enough to carry easily to work or school. These are the factors that make a bento a bento—it doesn't have to be a work of art using only Japanese recipes, nor should it be simply a thrown-together meal in a plastic container—and this is the philosophy that underpins all the recipes and ideas in this book.

Tips for Speedy Bento-making

How is it possible to assemble a varied, healthy bento box in twenty minutes or less in the morning? Here are my top tips for streamlining your morning bento-making routine.

Prepare as much as possible the night before
Cutting up vegetables, slicing meat, washing and drying greens—all of these can be done the night before, and will cut down on your bento-making time in the morning.

Make at least one bento item in advance
Having at least one of the dishes you plan to pack already made and ready to go can set your mind at ease. Instructions for the bentos in this book suggest which items can be made the night before or even further in advance.

Stock up on bento staples
Many bento-friendly foods can be made in advance and frozen or kept in the refrigerator or pantry. They only need heating up or quickly cooking to be ready to go. You'll find more information on making these foods in the Bento Staples section (page 118).

Make some "planned leftovers" for future bentos
Get into the habit of making "planned leftovers" when you prepare dinner. For instance, if you make a casserole, you can purposely set aside some to pack for lunch the next day or to freeze for a future bento. Another example of this strategy is to cut up twice as many vegetables as you need and store half of them for later use. This only takes a little additional effort, and saves a lot of time in the end.

Have everything ready to go
Before you go to bed, set out the bento box and accessories you plan to use, as well as the pots and pans and cooking utensils. Transfer any frozen foods you want to use to the refrigerator. If you're using a rice cooker, make sure it's switched on and the timer set to the proper completion time. Just a few minutes of preparation the night before will save lots of time in the morning and set your mind at rest too.

Invest in a rice cooker
If rice is a regular component of your bento, a rice cooker is an invaluable piece of kitchen equipment. The one essential feature to have is a timer function, which will allow you to set the cooker so that the rice finishes cooking in the morning, ready to pack. A good rice cooker can cook many other grains besides rice.

Don't overreach
Perusing bento blogs on the Internet can be intimidating if you are just starting out on your bento journey. Is it necessary to have rice balls with cute faces and

ham and cheese laboriously carved to look like anime characters to call your packed lunch a bento? Absolutely not—a bento is a meal first and foremost, not a craft project. Concentrate on assembling a few tasty, nutritious foods in your box first. The frills are just extra.

Use fresh fruit for the perfect dessert

Bentos that include things like sugarcoated chocolate candies just for the sake of their color don't appeal to me, and I usually don't have time to make a dessert just for my bentos. Fresh, seasonal fruit is sweet and healthy, and makes a perfect, easy dessert. Occasionally I may pack a cookie or two, or a tiny piece of a brownie, as a special treat!

Timelines

Most of the bento menus in the book are accompanied by a timeline, which allows you to estimate how much time to budget for assembling the bento in the morning. Some multitasking is required, but the tasks are staggered so that you aren't overwhelmed. Read the timelines through before tackling a bento so that you know what to do.

You'll see that most bentos require some advance preparation the night before, in some cases up to twenty or thirty minutes, but carrying out these tasks as you make dinner saves you more time overall. (For example, wash and chop up your bento vegetables and your dinner vegetables at the same time.) There are also some bentos that rely on items you have made in advance that are stocked in the freezer or refrigerator. While I'm making dinner, or when I have free time on the weekends, I often prepare dishes to freeze or refrigerate for later use.

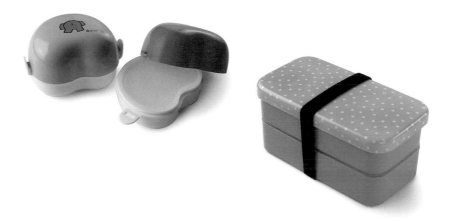

Bento Safety Tips

When you are preparing food that will be eaten some time after it's made, it's very important to follow some basic safety tips.

Practice good hygiene

Make sure the utensils and food containers that you use have been properly washed. Don't forget to wash your hands before making your bento! Try to avoid touching the food too much with your hands, especially in hot weather, since the more you handle food, the more chance you have of transferring undesirable bacteria onto it, no matter how carefully you wash your hands. Keep this in mind if you are making elaborately decorated bentos, and use chopsticks, tweezers, and other utensils to arrange the food whenever possible.

Be careful when you taste food. The standard way to taste in Japanese home kitchens is to put a little of the food you are preparing into a small bowl, and bring that to your lips, rather than sticking a spoon—or worse, your finger—into the pot.

Cool down cooked food before packing into a bento box

The condensation that forms in a closed container provides the moist warmth that harmful bacteria love. Make sure that the cooked food you pack, especially rice, has cooled down completely before the bento-box lid is closed.

Use an ice pack for certain foods, and in hot weather

Some foods, such as raw vegetables, and salads that use mayonnaise, need to be kept cooler than room temperature, especially in hot weather. There are many insulated bento boxes and lunch bags available. Some foods, such as fresh fruit, simply taste better when kept cool.

Do not use certain foods in bentos

Foods that should not be used in bentos include:

- Raw fish. Sushi made with raw fish is a no-no for bentos that you make in the morning and eat at lunchtime. See Egg-wrapped Sushi Bento (page 67) and Sushi Roll Bento (page 71) for examples of sushi that's safe for bentos.
- Undercooked meat, such as beef that is rare on the inside.
- Uncooked tofu. Moist, uncooked tofu is as liable to spoil as raw meat. Cooked tofu is fine.
- Egg that is not completely cooked, such as soft-boiled or runny poached eggs.
- Homemade mayonnaise, unless you can keep it very cool. Although commercial mayonnaise has preservatives, I prefer to ingest a few chemicals over getting sick. Homemade ranch and Thousand Island dressings, as well as tartar sauce, should be treated with similar care.
- Leftovers that seem a bit "off." This may seem obvious, but I have received emails over the years from people complaining that the days-old leftovers they packed for lunch went bad. However cute your bento box, it's not going to make bad food better. Please use common sense when it comes to food safety!

JAPANESE-STYLE BENTOS

In this section, I'd like to introduce you to some classic bento-box combinations that are favorites in Japan. With a few Japanese pantry staples, all of these can be made with ingredients that are easily available outside Japan.

Chicken and Three-color Pepper Stir-fry Bento

This beginner bento is made with everyday ingredients that you may already have in your pantry. It can be assembled in twenty minutes or less without any advance preparation. It's a good one to start your bento making adventures with.

Chicken and Three-color Pepper Stir-fry

1 SERVING

You can spice up this versatile and colorful stir-fry by adding some hot pepper sauce such as sriracha to taste. To ensure fast and even cooking, cut the peppers into small, regular cubes.

½ Tbsp olive or other vegetable oil
3 Tbsp roughly chopped green onion
2 tsp peeled and finely chopped fresh ginger
⅓ each medium-sized red, green, and yellow sweet peppers,
    de-seeded and cut into ½ inch (1cm) chunks
salt, for sprinkling
2 oz (60g) boneless, skinless chicken breast,
    cut into ½ inch (1cm) chunks
black pepper, to taste
1 Tbsp soy sauce
lettuce or shiso leaves used as dividers, optional

Heat the oil in a frying pan over medium heat. Add the green onion and ginger and stir-fry for 1–2 minutes until the oil is fragrant. Turn the heat up to the highest setting and add the peppers to the pan. Stir-fry with a spatula or long chopsticks. Sprinkle in some salt—this draws out moisture from the vegetables and cooks them a bit faster. Continue stir-frying for 4–5 minutes, until the peppers are cooked.

Push the vegetables to the sides of the pan, and add the chicken to the exposed bottom. Leave for a couple of minutes, then turn over to cook the other side. Stir everything together, and add black pepper and soy sauce.

Turn the stir-fry from the pan onto a cold plate so that it cools rapidly. When cooled, pack into the bento box, using the lettuce or shiso leaves as a divider.

AHEAD-OF-TIME NOTE: *Cut up the vegetables and chicken the night before, so everything is ready to just cook. Be sure to keep the raw chicken stored separately from the vegetables for safety.*

Instant Cabbage and Cucumber Pickles

1 SERVING

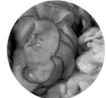

Instant or overnight pickled vegetables are very popular in Japan. They are like dressing-less salads, and the salty, slightly sour crunch provides a nice contrast to other foods. They can be eaten immediately or kept stored in the refrigerator for 3–4 days.

1 large green cabbage leaf
2 inch (5cm) length English cucumber, sliced into thin rounds
½ tsp sea salt
squeeze lemon juice

Cut out the tough vein of the cabbage leaf, and slice the rest into strips. Sprinkle the cabbage and cucumber with the salt, and massage well with your hands until the vegetables go limp. Let rest for at least 5 minutes. Add a squeeze of lemon juice.

Squeeze out any excess moisture before packing into a bento box. I like to put the pickles in a bento divider cup or cupcake liner (see page 116) to prevent the flavors from mingling with other flavors in the box.

Blanched Broccoli

Broccoli spears that have been blanched (quickly boiled then refreshed in cold water) are great for filling in gaps in the bento box, ensuring that the contents don't shift around. They're also good for you!

Put just enough water in a small pan to cover the broccoli. Bring the water to a boil, add a pinch of salt, and put in the broccoli florets (I usually just break them off the big broccoli head with my hands). Boil for 3–4 minutes, drain the water, and run cold tap water over the broccoli to cool quickly and fix the bright green color. Drain well.

TIME-SAVING NOTE: *You can use packaged frozen broccoli. Cook in the same way as raw broccoli, for 2–3 minutes.*

Basic White Rice

1 SERVING

This bento is made with 1 cup (200g) cooked Basic White Rice (see page 53).

Have hot precooked rice ready to go. Either set the timer on your rice cooker the night before so that the rice is ready in the morning or defrost some pre-cooked frozen rice in the microwave (see page 118). See this page for how to make great-tasting bento rice, and the facing for rice packing instructions.

Timeline

The timeline shows how to make all the components of your bento as efficiently as possible. Note that you can save even more time by prepping all of the vegetables the night before.

The timeline is for one bento. If you're making bentos for more than one person, add five minutes for each extra box.

Don't worry if you take longer than the timeline the first time you make a bento. The more bentos you make, the more efficient and speedy you'll be!

Great-tasting Bento Rice

Most Japanese bentos are constructed around plain steamed rice. Rice is not just a foil for the other food in a bento box, it's actually the star of the show.

Japanese style rice is slightly sticky and moist, with plump yet firm grains. For the best results, rice should be rinsed correctly, cooked fresh (see page 53), and packed while piping hot into your bento box. It should then be allowed to cool down to room temperature before the lid of the box is closed. In the olden days, Japanese mothers and grandmothers used to wake up at dawn to cook rice in a pot over a wood-burning stove; nowadays the electronic rice cooker with timer function has made making great-tasting rice for bentos in the morning a lot easier.

Even if you're using precooked and frozen rice (see page 118), for the best flavor it should be defrosted in the morning until hot, then allowed to cool down in the same way as freshly cooked rice. Heating up the frozen rice until hot makes it taste almost as if it's freshly cooked. Steamed rice does taste better if it's warm, so if you have access to a microwave oven at lunch-time, bring your bento in a heat-safe bento box and heat it up for a couple of minutes. If you are using a thermal lunch jar (see page 115), pack freshly cooked or defrosted piping hot rice into the preheated container, where it should keep warm for several hours.

TIMELINE

MINUTES	20	15	10	5	0
Rice (precooked)	☑ pack into bento box, let cool				
Chicken and Three-color Pepper Stir-fry	☑ cut up peppers, onion, ginger ☑ cut up chicken	☑ stir-fry onion, ginger	☑ sauté chicken, season ☑ stir-fry peppers	☑ take out and let cool	☑ pack into bento box with lettuce as divider
Instant Cabbage & Cucumber Pickles	☑ cut up cabbage and cucumber, massage with salt				☑ pack into cupcake liner
Blanched Broccoli	☑ boil water ☑ break off broccoli florets, put in pan	☑ drain broccoli, let cool			☑ pack into bento box with cherry tomatoes

Prep the night before: Set timer on rice cooker, if using.
Wash and dry lettuce to be used as divider.
Cutting up the vegetables and chicken the night before will save you 5 minutes in the morning.

How to Pack a Bento Box

Single-tier Box

1 Pack the rice into up to half of the bento box at the very beginning of the bento-making process so that it has time to cool down while you cook the rest of the bento contents. If you're in a hurry or the weather is hot, cool down the bento box fast by putting it on a cooler pack or a bag of ice while you prepare the rest of the bento. Use a spoon or rice paddle (moistened to prevent the grains from sticking) to pack the rice tightly so that it doesn't shift around during transit.

2 Fill half to two-thirds of the empty part of the box with your main dish—in this case, Chicken and Three-color Pepper Stir-fry. If your box has a divider, you can use it here between the rice and the other items to keep things looking neat. You can also use baran (plastic bento dividers), or make an edible divider with lettuce leaves, shiso leaves, or other broad-leafed vegetables.

3 Use a bento divider cup or cupcake liner to contain runny foods, or to separate foods whose flavors shouldn't mingle with other flavors in the box.

4 Finish by filling any gaps with broccoli florets or cherry tomatoes. This helps to prevent the bento-box contents from shifting around in transit, as well as making the box more colorful. Note that I've managed to get a lot of color into the box.

1

2

3

4

Two-tier Box

Two-tier boxes are even easier to pack than one-tier boxes. Two-tier boxes usually have a smaller capacity layer and a larger capacity layer. The rice usually goes into the larger capacity layer, but to cut down on the amount of rice I often put in a side dish, contained in a bento divider cup or cupcake liner. You may want to pack sauced or watery foods in the smaller capacity layer, which usually comes with its own sealed lid to prevent leaking.

TIP: *It's easy to vary the portion sizes for bentos. Just pick a larger box for a hearty appetite, a smaller box for a child or someone on a diet, and adjust the recipe quantities accordingly. See Bento Boxes and Accessories, page 114, for size guidelines.*

Tamagoyaki Bento

Tamagoyaki is a rolled omelette that is savory yet slightly sweet. It's such a popular bento item in Japan that many people insist on having a piece or two in their bento box every day! It may take a couple of tries to get the technique down, but you'll soon be rolling your own tamagoyaki with ease.

For this bento, everything else is prepped the night before so that you can concentrate on making a delicious tamagoyaki in the morning.

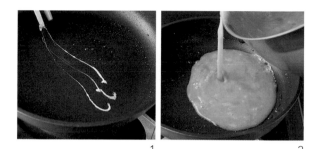

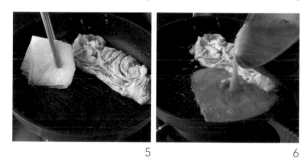

CONTENTS

Basic Tamagoyaki

2 SERVINGS

Tamagoyaki is traditionally made in a square pan dedicated to the purpose, but I always make mine in a regular 8 inch (20cm) diameter nonstick frying pan. It's possible to make a small, good-looking tamagoyaki with 2 eggs or even just 1 egg, but here I have used 4 eggs for 2 servings, since this is an easy amount for a beginner to roll into a nice shape. Tamagoyaki will keep in the refrigerator, well wrapped, for a day or two. Freezing will make the texture a little grainy and rubbery, though not inedible.

4 large eggs	½ tsp soy sauce
1 Tbsp sugar	vegetable oil, for frying
1 tsp mirin	parsley, for garnish
⅛–¼ tsp salt	

Mix together all of the ingredients, except for the oil, until the egg yolk and white are amalgamated, but not frothy.

Heat up the frying pan over medium-high heat. Pour in some oil and tilt the pan to spread it around. Take a small wad of paper towel and rub it around the pan to soak up any excess oil. Put the oil soaked wad on a small plate next to the stove.

Use cooking chopsticks or a fork to draw a little of the egg mixture along the bottom of the pan (1). If the egg cooks immediately, the pan is hot enough and ready to go. If the egg browns too fast, cool the pan down by putting the bottom on a moistened kitchen towel and lower the heat a little.

Pour a thin layer of the egg mixture into the hot pan (2). Tilt the pan to spread it around the bottom. Pierce any large bubbles that form with the chopsticks or fork.

As soon as the egg starts to set, start rolling it to one side of the pan. Flip one end over with the chopsticks or fork and keep flipping until you have a skinny roll. If you can't roll the egg you can just push it along to one side until you have a skinny little omelette (3–4).

Leaving the first roll at one side of the pan, rub the oil-soaked wad of paper towel firmly along the bottom of the pan. This adds just enough lubrication while also cleaning up any stray bits of egg (5).

Add a little more of the egg mixture to the pan, tilting the pan around to spread it (6). Lift the first roll up a little so that the uncooked egg runs beneath it (7, overleaf).

Puncture any large air bubbles that form, as before. As soon as this layer starts to set on top, roll it around the cooked egg roll to the opposite side of the pan (8, overleaf). As before, if the egg is browning too fast, place the pan on a moistened towel for a few seconds.

Repeat the preceding three steps until the egg mixture is all used up (9). The thinner the layers, the more delicately textured the tamagoyaki will be. Try to do a minimum of 4–5 layers.

When the tamagoyaki is done, turn seam-side down into the pan and press briefly to seal it. Flip the egg out onto a sushi mat or paper towel (10).

Roll the sushi mat or towel around the tamagoyaki, forming a rectangular shape (11). Leave to cool.

Cut into even slices before packing (12). Garnish with the parsley.

Don't despair if your tamagoyaki doesn't quite look perfect. It will still taste great!

7   8

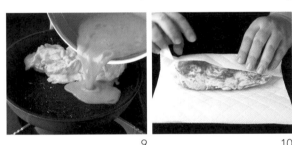

9   10

11   12

Ham and Cream Cheese Vegetable Rolls

1 SERVING

This is preferably made the night before and refrigerated, so that the cream cheese can firm up.

¼ small carrot	pinch salt
5–6 long, straight green beans, topped and tailed	2 slices ham
	2 Tbsp cream cheese, softened

Peel the carrot and cut into strips the same thickness and length as the green beans.

In a small pan, bring 1 inch (2.5cm) of water to a boil. Add a pinch of salt. Put in the carrot and green beans for 3–4 minutes, until crisp-tender. Drain, and cool rapidly under cold running water. Drain again and pat dry with kitchen or paper towels.

Set aside the 2 best looking strips of carrot and 3 straightest green beans. Cut up the rest to sprinkle on the rice.

Place a piece of plastic wrap on a flat surface, and lay 1 slice of ham on top of the plastic wrap so that a short side is closest to you. Spread the ham with all the cream cheese. Place the 2 strips of carrot and 3 green beans half an inch (1cm) from the edge closest to you. Roll the ham around the vegetables as tightly as you can, using the plastic wrap to aid you if needed. Roll the second slice of ham around the first roll. Wrap the roll tightly in plastic wrap and refrigerate overnight.

In the morning, unwrap the roll and cut into even pieces a little shorter than the height of the bento box.

Garlic Sautéed Spinach

1 SERVING

If you wash the leaves the night before, this can be made in a couple of minutes. The whole red chili pepper adds a hint of heat without overwhelming the other flavors.

Garlic-infused Olive Oil (see page 119), for frying	2 oz (60g) baby spinach leaves, washed and patted dry
1 small dried hot red chili pepper	salt and pepper, to taste

Heat the oil in a pan over medium-high heat. Add the chili, whole, and stir for a minute. Remove the chili and reserve.

Add the spinach and stir-fry rapidly. It will shrink down in mass in no time. Season with salt and pepper.

Turn out into a fine-mesh colander to drain off any excess moisture, and leave to cool. Pack into a bento divider cup or cupcake liner. Use the reserved whole red chili as decoration if you like—though you may want to leave it out if you think the bento recipient may eat it by mistake!

Basic White Rice with Mixed Vegetables

1 SERVING

Have hot precooked rice ready to go. Either set the timer on your rice cooker the night before so that the rice is ready in the morning or defrost some precooked frozen rice in the microwave (see page 118). See page 16 for how to make great-tasting bento rice, and page 17 for rice packing instructions.

1 cup (200g) cooked Basic White Rice (see page 53)
remaining green beans and carrot strips from Ham and Cream Cheese
  Vegetable Rolls, chopped

Pack the rice into the bento box and sprinkle with the
vegetables.

VARIATION RECIPES

Tamagoyaki

Tamagoyaki is a very versatile bento item that can be
used as the primary or secondary protein in your bento
box. Here are some of my favorite variations which
you can add to the Basic Tamagoyaki mixture on page
19. It's a bit harder to make thin layers when there are
additions to the egg mixture, so just try for 3 layers.

Green Onion Tamagoyaki
2 SERVINGS

2 Tbsp finely chopped green onion

Add the onion to the egg mixture. Roll and cook as
for the Basic Tamagoyaki.

Nori Tamagoyaki
2 SERVINGS

1 sheet nori seaweed, 7 x 8 inches (18 x 20cm), ripped or cut into fairly
  large pieces

Gently lay down a layer of nori on the top of each egg
layer as it cooks. The cut side of this tamagoyaki is
quite striking.

Furikake Tamagoyaki
2 SERVINGS

½ Tbsp furikake

Add your favorite furikake to the egg mixture. Cook
as for the Basic Tamagoyaki.

Parmesan Cheese and Parsley Tamagoyaki
2 SERVINGS

1 Tbsp Parmesan cheese, grated   ½ tsp finely chopped fresh parsley

Omit the sugar from the Basic Tamagoyaki mixture,
and reduce the salt by half, or omit it altogether if you
prefer. Add the cheese and parsley to the egg mixture. Cook as for the Basic Tamagoyaki.

Corn and Bacon Tamagoyaki
2 SERVINGS

1 slice bacon, finely chopped   1 Tbsp frozen corn kernels

Omit the sugar from the Basic Tamagoyaki mixture,
and reduce the salt to a pinch or omit it altogether if
you prefer. Sauté the bacon in a dry frying pan until
crispy. Drain off any excess fat and add the frozen
corn kernels to the pan; sauté until the corn has
defrosted, 2–3 minutes. Remove the bacon and corn
from the pan and beat into the egg mixture. Cook as
for the Basic Tamagoyaki.

TIMELINE

MINUTES	15	10	5	0
Rice (precooked)	☑ pack into bento box, let cool			☑ sprinkle cut-up vegetables on top
Ham and Cream Cheese Vegetable Rolls			☑ cut into pieces	☑ pack into bento box
Tamagoyaki	☑ beat egg mixture ☑ start to cook egg ☑ heat up frying pan	☑ turn out egg, roll up, and let cool	☑ cut into pieces	☑ pack into bento box with parsley
Garlic Sautéed Spinach		☑ put oil and chili in pan ☑ stir-fry spinach, season	☑ let cool	☑ pack into bento box

Prep the night before: Set timer on rice cooker, if using.
  Ham and Cream Cheese Vegetable Rolls.

Wash and dry spinach leaves.
Set out tamagoyaki-making equipment.

Fried Shrimp Bento

These Japanese-style breaded and deep-fried shrimps, known as *ebi furai* in Japan, are coated with panko breadcrumbs, which give a crispy texture. I like having deep-fried items once in a while for lunch, since they are so satisfying. Don't be afraid of the calories though—only a few shrimps are needed in a bento box, and here I've used plenty of vegetables to balance them out. There's also a little less rice than usual in this bento.

CONTENTS

- Breaded and Fried Shrimps
- Dipping Sauce of Your Choice
- Carrot and Celeriac Salad
- Radish Tulips
- Swiss Chard Namul
- Steamed Swiss Chard Stems with Butter
- Basic White Rice

Breaded and Fried Shrimps

1 SERVING

Deep-frying in lots of oil can be intimidating. This is only necessary, however, when you are cooking large amounts. Here only 3 shrimps are needed, so they can be shallow-fried in a small amount of oil—quicker to cook, and much easier to clean up afterwards.

Panko bread crumbs are now widely available, but if you can't get hold of any, fresh bread crumbs can be used. They will give a softer-textured coating.

3 large (16/20 count per lb or 40/50 count per kg) fresh or defrosted
    shrimps, shelled and deveined, tails left on
salt and pepper, to taste
2 Tbsp cornstarch
1 small egg, beaten
3 Tbsp panko bread crumbs
vegetable oil, for frying

Make tiny cuts along the inside of each shrimp (opposite to where the vein was) and gently pull the shrimp straight. This is an optional step, but it does make the shrimp look much bigger.

Pat the shrimps dry, and season with a little salt and pepper.

Put the cornstarch on one plate, the beaten egg in a small bowl, and the panko bread crumbs on another plate. Have another plate ready, lined with a couple of paper towels.

Heat ½ inch (1cm) of vegetable oil in a small frying pan over high heat. The oil is hot enough when a panko bread crumb dropped into it turns light brown right away.

Working rapidly, coat the shrimps in the cornstarch, dip in the egg, then roll in the bread crumbs. Try to do this with one hand, leaving the other hand clean to hold a pair of chopsticks or tongs to turn the shrimps. Gently put the shrimps one by one into the hot oil. Turn after a minute, and cook for another 30 seconds to a minute on the other side. The shrimps should feel firm when lightly tapped with the chopsticks.

As soon as each shrimp is cooked, remove from the oil and drain on the paper towels. When the last shrimp is removed from the oil, turn off the heat. If you're using an electric range, take the pan off the still-hot heating element for safety.

Leave the shrimps to cool thoroughly before packing into a bento box.

Put the dipping sauce of your choice in the sauce cup, to tuck into a corner of the bento box. Tartar sauce, mayonnaise, sriracha sauce, ketchup, Japanese brown sauce (sold as chuno or tonkatsu sauce), sweet chili sauce, and ranch dressing all go well with fried shrimps.

AHEAD-OF-TIME NOTE: *Bread the shrimps and freeze in a single layer, ideally on a metal baking sheet. (Metal conducts temperature much faster than plastic, so the shrimps will freeze faster.) Once the shrimps are frozen stiff, pack them in freezer bags or containers. Frozen breaded shrimps should be cooked for 2–3 minutes longer than fresh.*

TIP: *Make sure all the food in the bento box, especially the rice, has been thoroughly cooled to room temperature before packing the fried shrimps. Warm, moist rice will make the coating go soggy—though admittedly it will still be quite tasty, especially when it's drenched in sauce.*

Carrot and Celeriac Salad

8 SERVINGS

This is a refrigerator staple that lasts up to a week in a tightly covered container. I often make a batch to eat at home throughout the week, since it goes with meat, fish, or almost anything. The celeriac has such a distinctive flavor that no additional herbs are needed, but you can add a little fresh dill if you like.

1 large celeriac, peeled thickly to remove the knobby skin
2 large or 3 medium carrots
juice of 1 lemon
½ tsp sea salt
black pepper, to taste
1 tsp sugar
1 Tbsp olive oil

Slice the celeriac and carrots into long, thin shreds, using the shredder attachment of your food processor, or a mandoline, vegetable cutter, or grater.

In a bowl, toss the shredded vegetables with the other ingredients. Taste, and adjust the seasoning if needed. This can be eaten right away, but it will mellow a little as it rests.

Radish Tulips

These are very quick to make, and add some nice color to a bento.

Wash a small red radish and cut off the root and leaves, leaving a little of the leaf stems on for color. With a small, sharp knife, make zigzag cuts around the middle of the radish. Gently pull the radish halves apart. Sprinkle with a little salt to taste, if you like.

Radish tulips can be made a day in advance and stored in the refrigerator, covered tightly with plastic wrap.

Swiss Chard Namul

1 SERVING

In Japan, chard is called *fudanso*, meaning "everyday greens." Here I'm using the green leaves for one dish, and the white crunchy stems for another. *Namul* is a tasty Korean method of preparing vegetables that is very popular in Japan.

3–4 chard leaves, washed
1 tsp sesame oil
pinch sea salt
1 tsp white sesame seeds, toasted
pinch red chili powder, optional

Cut the chard leaves off the stems. Chop up the stems and reserve for the next dish.

Pour a full kettle of boiling water into a saucepan and turn the heat to high. Put the chard leaves in the boiling water for a minute, then drain. Run cold water over the leaves to cool them down rapidly and fix the vibrant green color. Drain the leaves, and squeeze them tightly to expel as much water as possible. Cut into bite-sized lengths.

Add the rest of the ingredients to the leaves and mix with your hands. Arrange in a cupcake liner or bento divider cup.

Steamed Swiss Chard Stems with Butter

1 SERVING

The stems of chard have a very different texture from the greens, and I've taken advantage of this to get two dishes out of one vegetable. Here the stems are steamed in the microwave or toaster oven. The toaster oven gives a slightly better, toasty flavor.

3–4 chard stems, roughly chopped
salt and pepper
½ tsp butter

Season the chopped-up chard stems with salt and pepper, and put the butter on top. Wrap in kitchen parchment paper if using a toaster oven, or place in a small bowl and cover with plastic wrap if using a microwave. Cook in a toaster oven at 400°F (200°C) for 8–10 minutes, or microwave on high for 4 minutes.

AHEAD-OF-TIME NOTE: *Both chard dishes can be made the night before. They will keep for 1–2 days in the refrigerator.*

Basic White Rice

1 SERVING

This bento is made with ¾ cup (150g) cooked Basic White Rice (see page 53).

Have hot precooked rice ready to go. Either set the timer on your rice cooker the night before so that the rice is ready in the morning or defrost some precooked frozen rice in the microwave (see page 118). See page 16 for how to make great-tasting bento rice, and page 17 for rice packing instructions.

VARIATION RECIPES
Shrimps

I think that shrimps always look so festive in a bento box. I usually have a bag of frozen uncooked shrimps in my freezer, and these come in very handy for bentos. The following recipes can be made with frozen peeled and deveined shrimps. The shrimps can be packed on a bed of rice as for the Breaded and Fried Shrimps (page 23), or to the side. Remember to let them cool before packing.

Lemon Butter Shrimps
1 SERVING

½ tsp butter
3 large, frozen shrimps
salt and black pepper, to taste
lemon juice, for sprinkling
slice lemon

Melt the butter in a small frying pan over medium heat. Add the frozen shrimps and the salt and pepper. Turn the heat to low, and cover. Steam-cook for 2 minutes, turn the shrimps over and cook for 2 minutes more. Sprinkle some lemon juice over the shrimps while they are still in the pan. Pack with a slice of lemon.

Salt and Pepper Shrimps
1 SERVING

olive oil, for frying
3 large, frozen shrimps
salt and black pepper, to taste

Put a small amount of olive oil in a pan over low heat. Add the frozen shrimps. Turn the heat to high and sauté on both sides for about 4 minutes, until the shrimps are no longer transparent. Season with the salt and a generous amount of black pepper.

Garlic Scented Shrimps
1 SERVING

½ Tbsp Garlic-infused Olive Oil (see page 119)
3 large, frozen shrimps
salt and black pepper, to taste

Heat the Garlic-infused Olive Oil (or half a finely chopped garlic clove with half a tablespoon olive oil) over medium-low heat. Add the frozen shrimps. Turn up the heat and sauté on both sides for about 4 minutes until the shrimps are no longer transparent. Season with salt and black pepper.

TIMELINE

MINUTES	15	10	5	0
Rice (precooked)	☑ pack into bento box, let cool			
Breaded and Fried Shrimps	☑ prep shrimps / ☑ prep egg/cornstarch/bread crumbs / ☑ heat oil ☑ fry shrimps		☑ drain and let cool	☑ pack sauce / ☑ pack into bento box on top of rice
Swiss Chard Namul	☑ boil water in electric kettle / ☑ cook leaves	☑ drain and let cool / ☑ mix with seasonings	☑ pack into bento box	
Steamed Swiss Chard Stems with Butter	☑ steam-cook stems	☑ let cool	☑ pack into bento box	
Carrot and Celeriac Salad, Radish Tulips			☑ pack salad in side box / ☑ cut radish	☑ put radish in bento box

Make in advance: Carrot and Celeriac Salad.

Prep the night before: Set timer on rice cooker, if using.
Put frozen shrimps in refrigerator to defrost.
Wash, dry, and cut up chard. Wrap stems with seasoning and butter in paper or put in bowl covered with plastic.

Mini-hamburger Bento

Meaty and satisfying, yet small and easy to pick up with chopsticks, mini-hamburgers are great for bento boxes, since they stay soft and juicy even when well cooked and cooled to room temperature. They are a great favorite with kids.

CONTENTS

- Mini-hamburgers
- Carrot and Cheese Flowers
- Red Onion and Parsley Salad
- Blanched Snow Peas
- Basic White Rice with Sesame Salt
- Fruit

Mini-hamburgers

6–8 SERVINGS (24 MINI-HAMBURGERS)

Japanese-style hamburgers are like round miniature meatloaves in flavor and texture, rather than all-beef American-style burgers, which can get tough when cold. These stay moist and flavorful, just like day-after meatloaf.

I have used a typical meatloaf mix of ground beef, pork, and veal, but you could use all beef instead. If using beef, choose one that is at least 10% fat (labeled "90% fat free") or your burgers may be rather dry.

The amounts given here make enough to stock extra mini-hamburgers in your freezer. I usually make these in advance, since dealing with raw ground meat first thing in the morning isn't something I like to do!

1 lb (450g) mixed ground beef, pork, and veal
⅓ cup (16g) fresh bread crumbs, or ⅓ cup (35g) dried bread crumbs and 2 Tbsp milk
1 medium onion, finely chopped, and sautéed in ½ Tbsp oil until translucent
1 egg
1 tsp salt
black pepper, to taste
½ tsp ground nutmeg
1 Tbsp vegetable oil
ketchup, steak sauce, tonkatsu sauce, or a mix, for coating

Put all the ingredients, except the oil and the ketchup, into a bowl and mix well with your hands until the meat is slightly sticky. Divide the mixture into 24 small, flattened balls.

Heat the oil in a large nonstick frying pan over medium-high heat. Put the mini-hamburgers in the pan in batches, with plenty of space around each one. Cook until browned on one side, then flip over, lower the heat and put a lid on the pan. Steam for 5–6 minutes until the hamburgers are cooked through: they will feel firm to the touch when done. Coat the hamburgers with a little ketchup or tonkatsu sauce, or a mix of both, before removing from the pan, and allow to cool completely before packing into a bento box or freezing.

To freeze the hamburgers, arrange in a single layer, ideally on a metal baking sheet. When frozen, pack into a freezer bag or box. Use within a month for optimum quality.

To use frozen precooked hamburgers, gently heat in a dry nonstick frying pan, covered, over medium-low heat for 8–10 minutes until warmed through. Alternatively, place on a microwave-safe plate and loosely cover with plastic wrap. Microwave on high for 4–5 minutes. Cool to room temperature before packing into a bento box.

Carrot and Cheese Flowers

1 SERVING

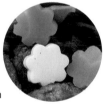

This garnish adds color as well as some extra nutrition and texture to the bento. If you can't be bothered to make cutouts, even adding some plain slices of carrot and cheese will make the presentation a little more special.

2 inch (5cm) length carrot, sliced into ¼ inch (0.5cm) rounds
cheese of your choice

Cut out decorative pieces from the carrot slices with a small cookie cutter, sugarcraft cutter, or bento cutter. Boil in salted water for 5 minutes or until the carrot slices are tender. Let cool before adding to the bento box.

To make cheese flowers, cut out shapes from sliced cheese. Cheeses that are easy to cut this way include Gouda, provolone, fontina, and Swiss. Presliced processed cheese will work too.

AHEAD-OF-TIME NOTE: *Cooked carrot cutouts freeze beautifully. Place in a single layer on a tray or plate, and freeze before packing into freezer bags. Just use the frozen cutouts as-is in a bento, where they will defrost by lunchtime, or heat them for a minute in the microwave before packing.*

TIME-SAVING NOTE: *You can use the water used to boil the carrot flowers to cook the Blanched Snow Peas (see below).*

Red Onion and Parsley Salad

1 SERVING

Massaging the raw onion with some salt takes away much of the harsh flavor of the onion slices, leaving them softened yet still crunchy—the perfect foil for the mini-hamburgers.

½ medium red onion, very thinly sliced
pinch salt
small bunch flat leaf parsley, finely chopped
black pepper, to taste
1 tsp rice vinegar
pinch sugar

Sprinkle the onion with a pinch of salt, and massage the salt well into the onion with your hands. The onion will exude a lot of moisture. Squeeze the onion to expel as much moisture as possible.

In a bowl, mix all the ingredients well. Pack into a cupcake liner or bento divider cup.

AHEAD-OF-TIME NOTE: *This salad can be made a day in advance and refrigerated, well covered.*

Blanched Snow Peas

1 SERVING

Vibrant green snow peas are a great bento garnish.

handful snow peas, topped and tailed, strings removed

Cook in boiling water for a couple of minutes, until crisp-tender. Drain, and cool rapidly under running water to fix the bright green color. Drain well before adding to the bento box.

Basic White Rice with Sesame Salt

1 SERVING

Have hot precooked rice ready to go. Either set the timer on your rice cooker the night before so that the rice is ready in the morning or defrost some precooked frozen rice in the microwave (see page 118). See page 16 for how to make great-tasting bento rice, and page 17 for rice packing instructions.

1 cup (200g) cooked Basic White Rice (see page 53)
Sesame Salt (see page 119), for sprinkling

Pack the rice into the bento box and sprinkle with the sesame salt.

TIMELINE

MINUTES	15	10	5	0
Rice (precooked)	☑ pack into bento box, let cool			☑ sprinkle with sesame salt
Mini-hamburgers	☑ reheat mini-hamburgers in frying pan or microwave	☑ let cool		☑ pack into bento box
Red Onion and Parsley Salad	☑ slice onions, chop parsley ☑ massage onion with salt	☑ mix with seasonings	☑ pack into bento box	
Blanched Snow Peas, Carrot and Cheese Flowers, Fruit	☑ cut out carrots and cheese	☑ cook carrots and snow peas ☑ let cool	☑ pack fruit into bento cup	☑ tuck snow peas into gaps in bento box

Make in advance: Mini-hamburgers.

Prep the night before: Set timer on rice cooker, if using.
Wash fruit, if necessary.
Trim snow peas, slice onion and massage with salt.

Mini-hamburgers

Mini-hamburgers fit nicely into a bento box and are easy to eat even for small children. They go well with rice or bread.

Nori-wrapped Mini-hamburgers
MAKES 24

Mini-hamburger ingredients (see page 27)
24 strips nori seaweed, 4 x 1 inch (10 x 2.5cm)
soy sauce, for drizzling

Make the mini-hamburgers as per the basic recipe, omitting the sauce. Before frying, wrap each hamburger with a strip of nori seaweed. When cooked, drizzle a little soy sauce on the surface of each hamburger while the pan is still hot.

Spicy Pork Mini-hamburgers
MAKES 24

Mini-hamburger ingredients (see page 27), using ground pork instead of the 3-meat mix
1 tsp peeled and grated fresh ginger
2 Tbsp chopped fresh coriander leaves
1 Tbsp saké
coriander leaves, for decoration
sriracha or hot chili sauce, for drizzling

Make the hamburgers as for the basic recipe, omitting the sauce, and add the ginger, coriander leaves, and saké. Before frying, stick a coriander leaf on each side of the mini-hamburgers. When cooked, drizzle a little sriracha or hot chili sauce into the pan and coat the mini-burgers in the sauce.

Bacon-wrapped Mini-hamburgers
MAKES 24

Mini-hamburger ingredients (see page 27)
12 slices bacon, halved crosswise
2 Tbsp honey or maple syrup, optional

Make the mini-hamburgers as per the basic recipe, omitting the sauce. Before frying, wrap each hamburger in half a slice of bacon. Pan-fry until the bacon is crisp and the meat is cooked through. To glaze the hamburgers, drain away the excess fat in the pan, and add honey or maple syrup. Turn the hamburgers until the honey or syrup is caramelized.

Tuna Mini-burgers
MAKES 24

14 oz (400g) water-packed canned tuna, well drained and flaked
1 Tbsp chopped fresh parsley
⅓ cup (16g) fresh bread crumbs, or ⅓ cup (35g) dried bread crumbs and 2 Tbsp milk
1 medium onion, finely chopped, and sautéed until translucent
1 egg
1 Tbsp mayonnaise
1 tsp salt
black pepper, to taste
1 Tbsp vegetable oil

Mix all the ingredients, except the oil, very well with your hands until everything sticks together, and form into mini-burgers. Fry on both sides over medium heat, turning gently so they don't fall apart.

Fresh Salmon Mini-burgers
MAKES 24

1 lb (450g) fresh, boneless, skinless salmon, chopped up in a food processor
⅓ cup (16g) fresh bread crumbs, or ⅓ cup (35g) dried bread crumbs and 2 Tbsp milk
3 Tbsp finely chopped green onion
1 egg
2 Tbsp chopped fresh dill
2 Tbsp cream cheese
butter and vegetable oil, for frying

Mix all the ingredients together very well with your hands until everything sticks together, and form into mini-burgers. Fry on both sides in a mixture of butter and vegetable oil over medium heat until just cooked through.

Vegan Black-bean Mini-burgers
MAKES 24

15 oz (425g) can black beans, drained and chopped up finely in a food processor
⅓ cup (16g) fresh bread crumbs from vegan bread
1 medium onion, finely chopped, sautéed until translucent
2 Tbsp chopped fresh coriander leaves
½ tsp ground cumin
1 tsp flour
½ tsp ground allspice
1 Tbsp vegetable oil

Mix all the ingredients, except the oil, very well with your hands to a pastelike consistency and form into mini-burgers, pressing each one together firmly. Pan-fry over low heat, turning gently so they don't fall apart. Pack some store-bought or homemade tomato salsa as a dip.

Ginger Pork Bento

This rich dish, consisting of slices of tender pork that are sautéed then coated in a ginger-scented sauce, is called *buta no shogayaki* in Japan, where it is a favorite for bentos and at-home meals. The braised new potato accompaniment is my invention, to use up as much of the delicious sauce as possible.

CONTENTS

- Ginger Pork with Braised New Potatoes
- Sweet Pepper and Bean Sprout Stir-fry
- Boiled Cauliflower with Mayonnaise
- Basic White Rice

Ginger Pork with Braised New Potatoes

1 SERVING

For the potatoes

5 tiny new potatoes, washed, unpeeled, and
   halved, or 1 medium regular potato, peeled
   and cut into bite-sized pieces
2 tsp butter
1 tsp soy sauce
sansho or black pepper, to taste

For the pork

vegetable oil, for sautéing
3 oz (90g) pork, in one piece or thinly sliced
½ Tbsp peeled and grated fresh ginger
2 tsp soy sauce
1 tsp saké
1 tsp mirin
lettuce to line the box

Put the potatoes in a pan and cover with cold water. Bring to a boil and cook for 5–6 minutes until tender but still firm. Set aside.

Heat a little vegetable oil in a nonstick frying pan over high heat. Quickly sauté each piece of pork on each side until browned, taking care not to overcook the meat. Remove the meat from the pan and wipe out the pan with a paper towel.

Put the ginger, the 2 teaspoons of soy sauce, the saké, and the mirin into the hot pan and let it come to a boil. Return the meat to the pan and coat with the sauce. Remove the meat.

Put the butter and boiled potatoes in the still-hot pan with the sauce. Add the 1 teaspoon of soy sauce. Toss the potatoes around to coat them thoroughly in the pan juices, then leave to braise over medium-low

heat for 5–6 minutes, turning occasionally until they turn a little crispy, while you make the other dishes that go into the bento. Sprinkle with sansho or black pepper.

Line the bento box with lettuce. Let the meat and potatoes cool completely before packing.

AHEAD-OF-TIME NOTE: *If you need to pound and slice the meat, do this the night before. Also, boil the potatoes the night before if you can, or use leftover cut-up potatoes.*

PORK NOTE: *For the juiciest results, use a cut of pork that is marbled with fat. My favorite is neck; shoulder works well too. Belly may be a little too fatty. Ginger pork made with very lean cuts such as loin may turn out rather dry. You can buy thinly sliced pork meant for stir-frying at Asian grocery stores and at many regular super-markets. You can also ask your butcher to slice it for you. If this is not possible, place the piece of pork in a sturdy plastic bag, and pound out thinly with a meat tenderizer or the broad side of a heavy knife, then cut into pieces.*

Sweet Pepper and Bean Sprout Stir-fry

1 SERVING

This crunchy, low-calorie dish is a great accompaniment to ginger pork. Since the ginger pork is quite strongly flavored, this is simply seasoned with salt and pepper.

oil, for frying
½ green or red sweet pepper,
   de-seeded and thinly sliced

1 cup (100g) bean sprouts, roots
   trimmed
salt and pepper, to taste

Heat a little oil in a small frying pan. Add the sweet pepper and sauté until slightly limp. Add the bean sprouts, and sauté for a few more minutes. Season with salt and pepper. Let cool before packing.

Boiled Cauliflower with Mayonnaise

1 SERVING

4–5 cauliflower florets
1 Tbsp mayonnaise
lettuce used as divider

Cook the cauliflower florets in boiling salted water until

just tender. Drain well and let cool. Pack with lettuce divider and the mayonnaise in a sauce cup.

Basic White Rice

1 SERVING

This bento is made with 1 cup (200g) cooked Basic White Rice (see page 53).

Have hot precooked rice ready to go. Either set the timer on your rice cooker the night before so that the rice is ready in the morning or defrost some precooked frozen rice in the microwave (see page 118). See page 16 for how to make great-tasting bento rice, and page 17 for rice packing instructions.

VARIATION RECIPES
Red, Yellow, and White Vegetable Sides

These vegetable sides add a splash of color to your bento, as well as being nutritious and tasty. Remember that in general, the more colorful a vegetable is, the more vitamins it has. The exception is the cabbage family, which tends to be pale in color but full of nutrition.

Honey-glazed Carrots

1–2 SERVINGS

1 medium carrot	salt and pepper, to taste
½ Tbsp honey	pinch ground cumin

Slice the carrot into any shape you like and boil until tender. Drain away most of the water until just a little is left, and add the honey. Season well with salt and pepper, and add a pinch of cumin. Stir around until the remaining moisture has evaporated. This keeps well in the refrigerator for 2–3 days.

Sautéed Cabbage with Cumin Seeds

1–2 SERVINGS

This is especially good if you can get hold of sweet spring cabbage.

1½ cups (100g) finely shredded cabbage
oil or butter, for sautéing
½ tsp cumin seeds
salt and pepper, to taste

Sauté the cabbage in the oil or butter until limp but still a little crisp. Add the cumin seeds. Season with salt and pepper.

Raw Beet Salad

1–2 SERVINGS

These days beets are available in many colors beyond the usual dark purple—yellow, white, even two-toned. Look for them at farmers' markets.

1 medium raw beet
1 Tbsp store-bought dressing of your choice

Peel, quarter, and slice the beet very thinly. Toss with dressing—ranch, French, and Thousand Island fit well.

Red and Yellow Peppers with Ketchup

1–2 SERVINGS

1 medium yellow sweet pepper, de-seeded and thinly sliced	½ tsp olive oil
	salt and pepper, to taste
1 medium red sweet pepper, de-seeded and thinly sliced	2 Tbsp ketchup

Sauté the peppers in the olive oil over high heat until crisp-tender. Season with the salt, pepper, and ketchup. Stir until the ketchup coats the peppers. (I know many people look down on ketchup these days, but I think it's still a very useful and tasty condiment!)

Curry-flavored Cauliflower

1–2 SERVINGS

This quick, curry-flavored sauté is a great way of livening up leftover cauliflower or any vegetable.

4–5 cauliflower florets, broken up into small pieces	½ tsp curry powder, mild or hot, to taste
1 tsp vegetable oil	salt and pepper, to taste

Boil the cauliflower until tender and drain well. Put the oil and curry powder in a pan over high heat and stir for 30 seconds. Add the cauliflower and toss. Season with salt and pepper.

Turnips Simmered in Stock

1–2 SERVINGS

3 small Japanese turnips or 1 medium Western turnip
dashi stock (see page 118), or chicken or vegetable stock, to cover
salt, to taste
sansho or black pepper, to taste

Peel and slice the turnips; if possible leave some of the green stalk on to add color. Simmer in the stock, seasoned with salt, until crisp-tender, 4–5 minutes for the Japanese turnips, 8–10 minutes for the Western one. Drain well and sprinkle with sansho or black pepper. Kohlrabi or rutabaga can be used instead of turnips.

Red Pepper and Onion with Miso and Sesame Seeds

1–2 SERVINGS

Miso not only adds lots of flavor, it makes a simple vegetable stir-fry quite hearty too. This keeps well in the refrigerator for 3–4 days, so make extra to use in several bentos throughout the week. For a spicy variation, add a de-seeded and finely diced fresh red chili pepper.

1 Tbsp white miso	1 large red sweet pepper, de-seeded and
1 Tbsp mirin	thinly sliced
1 tsp sugar	½ small onion, thinly sliced
1 Tbsp water	½ tsp soy sauce
1 tsp vegetable oil	1 Tbsp white sesame seeds

Combine the miso with the mirin, sugar, and water in a small bowl.

Heat up a frying pan or wok over high heat, and add the oil. Add the red pepper and the onion and stir-fry until the onion is translucent. Add the soy sauce and sesame seeds, then add the miso mixture. Stir rapidly for a minute to distribute the sauce and to

let the excess moisture evaporate. The sauce should start to caramelize almost immediately—be careful not to let it burn.

Baked Cherry Tomatoes with Pesto

1 SERVING

This quick tomato side dish, cooked in a toaster oven, makes a great little "sauce" to mix in with plain rice or pasta. If you use a conventional oven, you could make several at one time and freeze the extras.

2–4 ripe cherry tomatoes
1 Tbsp commercial pesto sauce
1 tsp grated Parmesan cheese

Cut the tomatoes in half and arrange in a small silicone or aluminum-foil bento divider cup. Cover with the pesto sauce, and sprinkle with the cheese. Bake in a toaster oven set to 400°F (200°C) for 8–10 minutes until bubbly. If using a conventional oven, preheat to 400°F (200°C) and bake for 10 minutes.

VARIATION: *Instead of pesto sauce, sprinkle a pinch each of salt, black pepper, and dried oregano on the halved cherry tomatoes. Drizzle on a teaspoon of olive oil, and sprinkle with grated cheese. Bake following the instructions above.*

TIMELINE

MINUTES	15	10	5	0
Rice (precooked)	☑ pack into bento box, let cool			
Ginger Pork	☑ heat up frying pan ☑ combine seasonings ☑ cook pork	☑ add seasonings	☑ remove pork and let cool	☑ pack into bento box with lettuce
Braised New Potatoes			☑ put potatoes in pork pan and braise ☑ let cool	☑ pack into bento box
Sweet Pepper and Bean Sprout Stir-fry	☑ stir-fry vegetables		☑ let cool	☑ pack into bento box
Boiled Cauliflower with Mayonnaise	☑ boil water	☑ cook cauliflower ☑ drain and let cool	☑ pack into bento box with lettuce divider ☑ put mayo or dressing into sauce container	

Prep the night before: Set timer on rice cooker, if using.
Pound pork and cut up, if needed.
Wash and trim bean sprouts; slice sweet pepper.

Boil the potatoes and cut up.
Wash lettuce or other greens used as dividers/liners.

Chicken Kara-age Bento

Chicken Kara-age (deep-fried marinated chicken) with a green onion sauce is the centerpiece of this bento.

Chicken Kara-age

1 SERVING

Chicken kara-age is deep-fried Japanese-style chicken, though its origins are Chinese. Boneless chicken pieces are marinated before being coated with cornstarch, resulting in a light and moist fried chicken that is deeply flavored. It's great hot or cold. You can omit the green onion sauce if you prefer.

For the chicken

4 oz (120g) boneless chicken thigh, with or without skin, cut into 3–4 pieces
1 tsp soy sauce (if you are not making the green onion sauce, increase to 2 tsp)
1 Tbsp saké
1 tsp peeled and grated fresh ginger
vegetable oil, for deep-frying
4 Tbsp cornstarch
handful arugula or other green salad leaves

For the green onion sauce

1 Tbsp rice vinegar
1 Tbsp soy sauce
1 Tbsp finely chopped green onion
pinch sugar
a few drops sesame oil
1 tsp peeled and grated fresh ginger

Combine the chicken, soy sauce, saké, and ginger. Let marinate for at least 10 minutes or overnight. (If you need to leave it marinating for more than 12 hours, omit the soy sauce and add it 10 minutes before cooking, or the salt will draw out too much moisture from the chicken and make it dry.)

Remove the chicken pieces from the marinade, drain, and coat in the cornstarch.

Heat 1 inch (2.5cm) of vegetable oil in a saucepan over medium-high heat. Test the oil temperature by putting a little of the cornstarch-and-marinade coating on the end of a wooden chopstick and dipping it into the oil. If the coating sizzles and turns brown immediately, the oil is hot enough. If the oil starts getting smoky, turn down the heat.

Fry the chicken pieces in the oil, turning once, until a deep golden brown. Drain well on paper towels.

To make the green onion sauce, combine all the ingredients in a small frying pan over medium heat and stir until the sugar is dissolved. Put the chicken pieces in the pan and toss to coat each piece with the sauce.

Let cool completely before packing into a bento box. Putting a layer of arugula or other salad leaves under the chicken enhances the color of the chicken and provides another texture in the bento.

AHEAD-OF-TIME NOTE: *You can cook chicken kara-age the night before. If I'm making this for dinner, I usually set aside a few pieces for the next day's bento.*

Chicken kara-age can be frozen uncooked and marinated, or cooked. To freeze it uncooked and marinated, put the chicken and marinade (excluding the soy sauce) into a freezer bag. Defrost in the refrigerator in a bowl, adding the soy sauce before frying. Cooked frozen pieces can be defrosted in the refrigerator, then crisped up for a few minutes in a toaster oven. I don't recommend defrosting cooked pieces in a microwave, since this will make the chicken tough.

Rice with Peas

1 SERVING

Have hot precooked rice ready to go. Either set the timer on your rice cooker the night before so that the rice is ready in the morning or defrost some precooked frozen rice in the microwave (see page 118). See page 16 for how to make great-tasting bento rice, and page 17 for rice packing instructions.

2 Tbsp frozen green peas
1 cup (200g) Basic White Rice (see page 53), warm

Put the peas in a small bowl with a pinch of salt and enough water to cover. Cover with plastic wrap, and microwave on high for 1 minute.

Mix into the rice with a spoon or rice paddle, taking care not to crush the peas.

Sweet Peppers Poached in Dashi Stock

1 SERVING

⅓ each yellow and red sweet pepper, de-seeded
1 cup (240ml) dashi stock (see page 118), or chicken stock
salt, to taste

Cut the sweet peppers into slices or shapes. Place in a small pan, and add enough dashi or chicken stock to cover; add salt to taste. Heat on high until the stock is bubbling, then lower the heat and gently simmer for 4–5 minutes until the pepper pieces are tender.

Here I have used pieces cut out with a small rabbit-shaped cookie cutter. The leftover bits of sweet pepper don't go to waste—I just chop them up finely and mix them in with the rice.

AHEAD-OF-TIME NOTE: *Make more of these decoratively cut peppers than you need, and freeze the extras. Pop a few into a bento box whenever you need a little extra color.*

Blanched Spinach with Sesame Sauce

1 SERVING

This is usually made with sesame seeds that are ground in a Japanese mortar (*suribachi*), which has a ridged, ceramic surface, and pestle (*surikogi*). Here is a simplified version that uses tahini, but I have included optional instructions for a traditional sesame sauce. The traditional sauce does taste a little better, but takes more time and effort.

3½ oz (100g) spinach leaves, washed
1 Tbsp tahini, nerigoma, or Traditional Sesame Sauce (see this page)
½ tsp white sesame seeds, toasted
1 tsp sugar
½ Tbsp soy sauce
½ tsp white sesame seeds, toasted, for sprinkling

Boil the spinach for 1 minute. Drain, then fill the pan with cold water, repeating until the spinach is cooled. Squeeze out as much water as possible from the cooked spinach, then form it into a log shape. Cut the spinach into even pieces.

In a small bowl, mix together the tahini, ½ teaspoon of toasted white sesame seeds, sugar, and soy sauce, pressing down to grind up the sesame seeds and sugar slightly. Add the spinach and mix well. Pack into your bento box and sprinkle with sesame seeds.

Traditional Sesame Sauce

1 SERVING

For this recipe you should ideally use a mortar that will be large enough to hold the spinach when it is added after making the sauce.

2 Tbsp white sesame seeds, toasted
1 tsp sugar
½ Tbsp soy sauce

Put the sesame seeds and sugar into the mortar. Grind well with the pestle, until the sesame seeds are crushed and smell very nutty. Add the soy sauce and mix well. Add the cooked and chopped spinach and combine with the sesame sauce.

AHEAD-OF-TIME NOTE: *Make single-size portions of Blanched Spinach with Sesame Sauce, place in cupcake liners or bento divider cups, and freeze. You can pack a frozen cup of spinach directly into a bento box—it will be defrosted and ready to eat by lunchtime, unless the bento is in a very cold location.*

VARIATION RECIPES
Quick Green-vegetable Sides

Green vegetables are not only full of vitamins and minerals, they provide a great splash of color in a bento box. Generally speaking, the darker the green, the more nutritious the vegetable.

Green Asparagus with Sesame Sauce
1 SERVING

4–5 medium asparagus spears
1 Tbsp Traditional Sesame Sauce (see above)

Cut off and discard the woody stem ends of the asparagus, and cut the remainder into bite-sized pieces. Boil for 4–5 minutes until tender, drain, and run cold water over them to fix the green color. Drain well, and mix with Traditional Sesame Sauce (see above). This sauce can be used for any cooked vegetable. I love it with green beans or with okra.

Green Beans with Pine Nuts and Miso
1–2 SERVINGS

1 Tbsp pine nuts
large handful green beans

½ Tbsp mild white miso
1 tsp butter

Put the pine nuts in a small, dry, nonstick frying pan over high heat. Stir for 3–4 minutes until lightly toasted. Remove from the pan and set aside. Top and tail the green beans and cut into 1 inch (2.5cm) pieces. Put the green beans in the same pan with just enough water to cover. Turn up the heat and "sauté" in the water until the beans are crisp-tender. Drain off any excess water, then return the green beans to the pan over medium-low heat. Add the miso and the butter and stir until the green beans are coated. Add the pine nuts and mix. Leftovers can be kept in the refrigerator for 1–2 days. I like this so much that I don't mind packing this whole amount in my bento, with just tamagoyaki and rice.

Broccoli with Grainy Mustard
1 SERVING

2–3 broccoli florets
½ Tbsp grainy mustard
½ tsp lemon juice
pinch sugar

Boil the broccoli until tender, then let cool. Combine the rest of the ingredients, then mix with the cooled broccoli.

Microwave-steamed Baby Bok Choy with Oyster Sauce
1 SERVING

leaves of 2 baby bok choy, separated
salt and pepper, to taste
1 Tbsp oyster sauce

Place the bok choy leaves on a microwave-safe plate in a single layer, sprinkle with salt and pepper, and cover with plastic wrap. Microwave on high for 3–4 minutes, until the leaves are limp. Take out, drain off excess moisture, and add the oyster sauce. Mix on the plate to combine. Return to the microwave and cook for another 30 seconds. Let cool before packing into a bento box.

Garlic-sautéed Broccoli Rabe
2 SERVINGS

1 cup (40g) roughly chopped broccoli rabe or sprouted broccoli
Garlic-infused Olive Oil (page 119), for frying
salt and pepper, to taste

Stir-fry the broccoli in the Garlic-infused Olive Oil over medium-high heat for 4–5 minutes, until crisp-tender. Season with salt and pepper. Leftovers will hold in the refrigerator for 1–2 days.

TIMELINE

In this timeline, I've suggested making almost everything in advance, leaving just the addition of peas to the rice, cooking the chicken, and dressing the spinach for the morning. You could make the chicken kara-age in advance if you prefer, though I think it tastes best if you can manage to make it in the morning.

MINUTES	20	15	10	5	0
Rice (precooked) with Peas	☑ microwave frozen peas	☑ pack into bento box, let cool ☑ mix into rice			
Chicken Kara-age	☑ heat up pan with oil ☑ coat chicken in cornstarch		☑ fry chicken ☑ make green onion sauce	☑ drain and toss in sauce ☑ let cool	☑ pack into bento box on greens
Blanched Spinach with Sesame Sauce				☑ make sesame sauce and mix with spinach	☑ pack into cup and into box
Sweet Peppers Poached in Dashi					☑ pack into bento box

Prep the night before: Set timer on rice cooker, if using. Sweet Peppers Poached in Dashi Stock. Wash and cook spinach.
Wash and dry greens to line bento. Marinate chicken.

Mixed-vegetable Rice and Salted Salmon Bento

A trio of traditional favorites—steamed rice with mixed vegetables; simply grilled, presalted salmon fillets; and sweet-salty simmered kabocha squash—make up this classic bento. The combination of salty and sweet flavors is quintessentially Japanese.

CONTENTS

Mixed-vegetable Rice

4 SERVINGS

This style of rice dish, which is steamed with various ingredients and seasonings, is called *takikomi gohan* in Japanese. This version has carrots, dried shiitake mushrooms, and burdock root, turnip, or parsnip. Leftovers can be frozen for later use.

½ medium carrot
4 inch (10cm) length burdock root,
     or equivalent amount of turnip or parsnip
2 dried shiitake mushrooms
1½ cups (300g) or 2 rice-cooker cups uncooked white rice, rinsed (see page 53 for rinsing instructions)
2 Tbsp saké
2 Tbsp soy sauce
⅛ tsp salt
1.8 cups (430ml) or 2¼ rice cooker cups soaking liquid from the shiitake mushrooms

At least an hour ahead, or the night before, soak the shiitake in enough water to completely immerse them—at least 1.8 cups (430ml). Remove from the water, reserving the soaking liquid. Squeeze out excess moisture from the shiitake, discard the stems, and chop the caps finely.

Peel and finely shred the carrot and the burdock root, turnip, or parsnip. Slice the shiitake into thin strips.

If cooking on the stove top, put all the ingredients into a heavy-bottomed pot and stir. Bring to a boil, cover, and lower the heat. Simmer for 15–20 minutes until the water has gone and little holes develop all over the surface of the rice. Turn off the heat and leave the rice to steam, covered, for at least 10 minutes. If using this method, make in advance and freeze until ready to use.

If using a rice cooker, put all the ingredients in the rice cooker the night before. Set the timer so that the rice finishes cooking in the morning.

With either method, the vegetables may float to the top of the rice while cooking. Fluff up the rice and mix the vegetables back in with a rice paddle before packing.

Grilled Salted Salmon

1 SERVING

2½ oz (70g) slice salted salmon, store-bought or homemade (see below)

Heat up a nonstick frying pan or grill. Place the salted salmon in the pan or grill—there's no need to oil the pan, since the salmon itself is quite oily. Cook until very lightly browned on one side, then turn over and cook for a couple of minutes more.

Alternatively, place the salmon on aluminum foil and bake in a toaster oven for 5 minutes on one side, 3 minutes on the other.

Homemade Salted Salmon

MAKES 4 BENTO-SIZED FILLETS, 2½ OZ (70G) EACH

In Japan, salted, half-cured salmon (*shiozake*) is as popular and ubiquitous as smoked salmon in the West. Salted salmon fillets cook up fast, keep longer than fresh salmon, and require little or no additional seasoning. Although cheap and easily available in Japan, they are quite expensive in other countries, and only available at Japanese groceries. They are not difficult to make in the refrigerator, however. Just make sure you start with very fresh salmon. I prefer to use wild salmon over farmed, since the latter tends to be very fatty.

10 oz (280g) very fresh boneless salmon with the skin on
finely ground or flaked noniodized sea salt, about 4 tsp

Cut the salmon into 4 pieces crosswise. Salt each piece on both sides rather heavily (½–1 teaspoon of salt per piece). Lay the pieces in a nonreactive plastic or bamboo colander. Put the colander on a plate to catch any drips. Place the colander and plate in the refrigerator. If the fish is fresh it shouldn't make your refrigerator smell.

Leave in the refrigerator for 2–3 days, turning the pieces over when you remember to (about 3–4 times).

At the end of the process, the salmon will have shrunk slightly and turned a brighter shade of orange-pink. Wipe off any excess salt or moisture with paper towels. The fillets can be used right away, or will keep in the freezer, well wrapped, for up to 3 months. Wrap each fillet individually before freezing so that they are easy to take out and use for bentos. If stored in the refrigerator they should be used within 2–3 days.

Simmered Kabocha Squash

6 SERVINGS

This is a classic homey dish in Japan. Kabocha squash has a sweet taste and floury texture. If you can't find it, try substituting peeled butternut squash or even sweet potato. Regular pumpkin (the kind used to carve jack-o'-lanterns) is too watery and fibrous.

3 cups (345g) kabocha squash, unpeeled, and cut into bite-sized pieces
1 cup (240ml) dashi stock (see page 118)
2 Tbsp saké
2 Tbsp mirin
1½ Tbsp sugar
1½ Tbsp soy sauce
pinch salt

Take little bits of the outer skin off each piece of the squash randomly, or in a decorative pattern, with a knife or peeler. This helps the squash pieces to cook faster.

Put all the ingredients in a saucepan and bring to a boil. Lower the heat and simmer for about 20 minutes, turning the kabocha pieces from time to time, until the liquid has reduced to half. Leave the kabocha to cool in the liquid; it will absorb flavor as it cools. Drain well before packing.

This will keep in the refrigerator for 3–4 days. To freeze, divide into single portions of 2–3 pieces and place each portion in a cupcake liner. Freeze on a tray. Once frozen, pack into a freezer bag. Defrost the single portions in the microwave on high for a couple of minutes, and let cool before packing.

Blanched Green Beans

1 SERVING

Since the other dishes in this bento are well flavored, I've kept the green beans simply flavored with salt. Cook together with the edamame.

handful green beans, topped and tailed
pinch salt

Put the green beans in a pan with water to cover, and add the salt. Boil until crisp-tender. Drain, cool, and cut to an attractive size before packing.

Blanched Edamame Beans

1 SERVING

This is a simple, yet colorful and nutritious garnish.

handful frozen, shelled edamame beans

Toss the edamame into the water with the green beans. Scatter on top of the rice.

Alternatively, you can cook the edamame with the rice, but this will dull the color of the beans. I prefer to cook them separately.

VARIATION RECIPES
Mixed-rice Dishes

The mixed-rice dishes known as *takikomi gohan* in Japanese can be a great way to appreciate the flavor and texture of a single seasonal ingredient, such as chestnuts or bamboo shoot. Or, you can include all kinds of vegetables and meat to make a one-dish meal. Mixed rice is as easy to make as plain rice in a rice cooker, and is quite healthy since it usually has little or no added fat, compared to pilaus and risottos.

To cook these dishes, follow either the stovetop method or the rice-cooker method on page 39.

Five-ingredient Rice with Chicken
4 SERVINGS

This classic rice dish, with five main ingredients added to the base of rice and seasonings, is known as *gomoku gohan* in Japanese, which literally means "five-ingredient rice." A bento box filled just with this rice makes a very satisfying lunch.

1½ cups (300g) or 2 rice-cooker cups uncooked rice, rinsed (see page 53 for rinsing instructions)
1.8 cups (430ml) or 2¼ rice-cooker cups dashi stock (see page 118)
2 Tbsp soy sauce
1 Tbsp saké
1 Tbsp mirin
¼ tsp salt
1 cup (130g) finely chopped carrot, burdock root, fresh shiitake, and daikon radish
3 oz (90g) chicken, ground or cut into small dice

Chestnut Rice

4 SERVINGS

This is a great autumnal dish, and very filling too—perfect for hearty appetites.

1½ cups (300g) or 2 rice-cooker cups uncooked rice, rinsed (see page 53 for rinsing instructions)
1.8 cups (430ml) or 2¼ rice-cooker cups dashi stock (see page 118)

½ tsp sea salt
1 tsp mirin
10 oz (280g) whole boiled or roasted chestnuts

Mushroom Rice

4 SERVINGS

Another dish that is popular in the fall, when abundant varieties of mushrooms are in season. Use whatever fresh mushrooms are available to you. The wild varieties have more flavor than cultivated ones.

2 cups (150g) combined sliced fresh mushrooms (shiitake, oyster, chanterelle, maitake, etc.)
2 Tbsp soy sauce
1 Tbsp saké
1 Tbsp mirin
pinch salt

1½ cups (300g) or 2 rice-cooker cups uncooked rice, rinsed (see page 53 for rinsing instructions)
1.8 cups (430ml) or 2¼ rice-cooker cups dashi stock (see page 118)

Put the mushrooms in a bowl with the soy sauce, saké, mirin, and salt and massage the seasonings into the mushrooms with your hands before cooking with the rice.

Bamboo-shoot Rice

4 SERVINGS

In Japan, bamboo shoots are a harbinger of spring, and this subtly flavored rice is one of the best ways to enjoy them. By using precooked bamboo shoot, this dish becomes as easy to make as plain rice. I prefer vacuum-packed bamboo shoot over canned because I think it has a better texture and flavor.

1½ cups (300g) or 2 rice-cooker cups uncooked rice, rinsed (see page 53 for rinsing instructions)
1.8 cups (430ml) or 2¼ rice-cooker cups dashi stock (see page 118)

1 Tbsp saké
1 Tbsp sea salt
1 cup (120g) precooked bamboo shoot, cut into bite-sized pieces

Carrot Rice

4 SERVINGS

This bright orange rice is a great way to sneak some extra vegetables into your kids' bentos. If they don't like the flavor of dashi stock, use vegetable stock instead. I use a food processor to shred the carrot fast.

1½ cups (300g) or 2 rice-cooker cups rice, rinsed (see page 53 for rinsing instructions)
1.8 cups (430ml) or 2¼ rice-cooker cups dashi stock (see page 118)
1 cup (110g) grated or shredded carrot
1 Tbsp butter

When the rice is cooked, mix in the butter.

TIMELINE

MINUTES	10		5	0
Mixed-vegetable Rice (precooked)	☑ pack into bento box, let cool			
Grilled Salted Salmon	☑ heat up pan or grill	☑ grill salmon	☑ let cool	☑ pack into bento box
Simmered Kabocha Squash	☑ defrost in microwave		☑ let cool	☑ pack into bento box
Blanched Green Beans and Edamame, Tomato & Parsley	☑ cook green beans and edamame		☑ drain and let cool	☑ pack into bento box, garnish with tomato and parsley

Make in advance: Mixed-vegetable Rice (if using stovetop method).
Simmered Kabocha Squash.
Homemade Salted Salmon.

Prep the night before: Prep rice and set timer on rice cooker, if using.

Soboro Bento

Soboro is finely chopped or ground meat, fish, egg, or vegetables, seasoned and served mixed in with or sprinkled onto rice. One, two, or more kinds of soboro, served with rice, make a great "one-pot" bento.

CONTENTS

Turkey Soboro

6–8 SERVINGS

Meat soboro can be made with any kind of finely chopped or ground meat. Here I have used turkey. Note that with a low-fat meat like turkey, you need to add plenty of flavors to make the meat as tasty as possible. It's also important to stop cooking while there is still some cooking liquid, to keep the meat moist. I like to make this in quantity and freeze the extra for future bentos.

1 lb (450g) turkey or chicken, finely ground
2 tsp peeled and grated fresh ginger
4 Tbsp saké
4 Tbsp mirin
¼ cup (60ml) chicken stock
2 Tbsp soy sauce
½ tsp salt
2 Tbsp sugar
beni shoga or gari pickled ginger, for garnish

Put all the ingredients in a saucepan over medium heat. Using two pairs of wooden or bamboo chopsticks held together, keep stirring the meat mixture as it cooks. (Using two pairs of chopsticks makes the meat more finely grained. You can also use two forks held together.) The liquid will gradually evaporate. Keep mixing vigorously to keep the meat from clumping. Remove from the heat when the liquid is almost gone, but before the pan is totally dry. Let cool before packing. Garnish with pickled ginger.

This keeps in the refrigerator, well covered, for a week, and in the freezer for up to a month. Just divide into individual portions and store pressed flat in freezer bags.

Egg Soboro

1 SERVING

Egg soboro, called *iritamago* in Japanese, is a versatile dish that can be used on rice, noodles, in stir-fries, and more. I like to make this dish fresh for each use, but you can make it in some quantity and freeze it, to save time.

1 egg
½ tsp sugar
pinch salt
1 tsp saké, optional

Beat all the ingredients together in a bowl. Pour into a small pan over medium heat. Using two pairs of wooden or bamboo chopsticks held together, or two forks, keep stirring the egg mixture vigorously as it cooks to form fine granules. It should look like dry scrambled egg. As soon as the egg mixture has cooked, remove from the heat. Let cool before packing.

Carrot Soboro

2–4 SERVINGS

Carrot soboro can be frozen for up to a month.

1 large carrot, finely shredded
¼ cup (60ml) dashi stock (see page 118)
1 tsp mirin
pinch salt
1 tsp soy sauce
½ tsp sugar

Put all the ingredients in a small pan and bring to a boil over high heat. Lower the heat and simmer for 4–5 minutes until the carrot is tender. Drain and cool before packing.

Green Bean Soboro

1 SERVING

Chop up some fresh or frozen green beans, and boil in salted water until crisp-tender.

Basic White or Brown Rice

1 SERVING

This bento is made with 1 cup (200g) cooked Basic White or Brown Rice (see page 53).

Have hot precooked rice ready to go. Either set the timer on your rice cooker the night before so that the rice is ready in the morning or defrost some pre-cooked frozen rice in the microwave (see page 118). See page 16 for how to make great-tasting bento rice.

TO ASSEMBLE THIS BENTO

Put half of the cooked, warm rice in the bento box. Put half of each soboro mixture on top of the rice—this layer doesn't have to be neat since it will be hidden. Cover with the rest of the rice. Arrange the rest of the soboro in a neat pattern on top. Finish with some chopped beni shoga or gari pickled ginger.

VARIATION RECIPES

Soboro

Soboro can be made with all kinds of things; most of the alternatives listed below freeze well too. Armed with some soboro and rice, you can assemble a satisfying bento in no time.

Beef Soboro

6–8 SERVINGS

1 lb (450g) finely ground lean beef
1 Tbsp peeled and chopped fresh ginger
4 Tbsp saké
4 Tbsp mirin
¼ cup (60ml) chicken stock
4 Tbsp soy sauce, or 2 Tbsp soy sauce and 2 Tbsp oyster sauce
2 Tbsp sugar
1 tsp sesame oil, optional
pinch red chili flakes, optional

Cook as per the instructions for Turkey Soboro (page 43). You can use ground pork, veal, or even buffalo or ostrich instead of beef.

Western-flavored Soboro

6–8 SERVINGS

oil, for sautéing
½ cup (65g) finely chopped mixed vegetables, such as carrot, sweet pepper, or celery
1 lb (450g) finely ground beef, pork, veal, or combination of the three
½ cup (120ml) chicken or veal stock
3 Tbsp white wine
1 tsp salt
1 shallot, finely chopped
1 tsp dried thyme

Use this soboro when you want a more European or Western flavor. Sauté the vegetables in a little oil until limp, and add the meat and the rest of the ingredients. Stir over medium heat, breaking up clumps, until the liquid is just about gone. This soboro makes a great filling for omelettes, and can be mixed into pasta too.

White Fish Soboro

2–4 SERVINGS

I've used cod here, but any flaky white fish can be used, such as striped bass, white sea bass, haddock, or tilapia.

7 oz (200g) cod, fresh or frozen
3–4 cups (720–960ml) dashi stock (see page 118)
2 Tbsp saké
1 Tbsp mirin
1 Tbsp soy sauce
1 tsp peeled and grated fresh ginger
½ tsp salt
2 tsp sugar

If the fish needs to be defrosted, transfer it from freezer to refrigerator the night before, or up to 24 hours in advance of cooking.

Place the fish in a pan with enough dashi stock to cover, bring to a slow boil, then lower the heat to a simmer. Cook until the fish loses its transparency. Take out the fish, and pour the dashi out into a bowl. Debone, skin, and flake the fish roughly.

Put ½ cup (120ml) of the reserved dashi and the rest of the ingredients, except the fish, into the pan. Bring to a boil. Lower the heat and add the flaked fish. Cook over medium-low heat, stirring and continuing to flake the fish finely, until the moisture is gone.

Tofu Soboro

4–6 SERVINGS

This classic tofu dish is known by the name *iridofu* in Japan. It takes a few more steps to make than the other soboro recipes, but is well worth the effort. It's an ideal protein for vegetarians, but omnivores love it too!

4 dried shiitake mushrooms

1 lb (450g) firm tofu

2 Tbsp mild white miso

1 Tbsp soy sauce

1½ cups (240g) finely chopped green onion

1 tsp peeled and finely chopped fresh ginger

2 Tbsp sesame oil

⅓ tsp salt

sansho or black pepper, to taste

At least an hour ahead or the night before, soak the shiitake in enough water to completely immerse them. Remove from the water, reserving the soaking liquid. Squeeze out excess moisture from the shiitake, discard the stems, and chop the caps finely.

Take the tofu out of its container and drain off all the water. Place in a fine-mesh colander, and put a weight on top (for example, a plate with a can on top). Leave to drain until the tofu has reduced in mass to about a third of its original size.

Alternatively, put the drained tofu on a plate, and put another plate on top. Microwave for 5 minutes until the tofu has reduced in mass to about a third. Drain off the water that has accumulated on the bottom plate.

In a small bowl, combine the miso, soy sauce, and about 4 tablespoons of the shiitake soaking liquid to make a smooth paste.

In a large frying pan, briefly sauté the chopped shiitake, green onion, and ginger in the sesame oil over high heat. Lower the heat to medium. Add the tofu to the pan, crumbling it with your hands. Add the salt. Keep stirring the tofu, using two pairs of cooking chopsticks held together or two forks, until it starts to resemble fine, rather dry scrambled eggs.

Add the combined miso, soy sauce, and shiitake soaking liquid to the pan and continue stirring until the liquid is completely absorbed and the pan is dry. Sprinkle with a little sansho or black pepper.

Let cool completely before packing. This dish is best made the night before. It can be stored in the refrigerator for up to a week. It does get a little tough if it's been frozen, though it's still pretty good.

Tuna Soboro
2–4 SERVINGS

7 oz (200g) canned tuna, well drained

2 Tbsp saké

1 Tbsp soy sauce

1 Tbsp chopped green onion

1 Tbsp peeled and grated fresh ginger

Flake the tuna into a pan and add the other ingredients. Cook over medium heat, stirring and breaking up the tuna, until the liquid is just about gone but the tuna is still moist. Be careful not to overcook this, especially if you are using water-packed tuna.

TIMELINE

For quick assembly, I recommend making the Turkey Soboro in advance and freezing, and the Green Bean Soboro and the Carrot Soboro the night before. The only thing I recommend making in the morning is the Egg Soboro.

MINUTES	10	5	0
Turkey Soboro	☑ defrost		
Egg Soboro	☑ beat egg mixture		
		☑ make Egg Soboro	
Assemble soboro bento with precooked rice		☑ layer rice and soboro	
			☑ let cool, garnish with ginger
Fruit		☑ cut up fruit if necessary	☑ pack into bento box

Make in advance: Turkey Soboro.

Prep the night before: Set timer on rice cooker, if using. Green Bean Soboro. Carrot Soboro.

Wash fruit, if necessary. Transfer frozen Turkey Soboro to refrigerator.

Chicken Kijiyaki Bento

What could be more appetizing than juicy chicken slices, burnished crispy brown? This is another favorite bento combination in Japan. The chicken is accompanied by sweet potato slices that are pan-steamed very simply, and a crunchy, fresh salad of pickled vegetables.

CONTENTS

Chicken Kijiyaki

1 SERVING

Kijiyaki refers to a traditional way of cooking bland foods such as chicken or tofu so that they supposedly mimic the taste of blue pheasant (*kiji*), a hunters' favorite and great delicacy in feudal Japan. The cooking method is basically the same as for teri-yaki—the only difference that I know of is that chicken kijiyaki is cooked to ensure the skin is crispy, and is sprinkled with spicy shichimi pepper. Either way, it's great when cooled, so it's a perfect bento dish.

4 oz (120g) boneless chicken thigh with skin
1 Tbsp mirin
1 Tbsp soy sauce
1 tsp sugar
shichimi pepper, to taste

Pierce the chicken all over on the skin side with a fork. This helps the meat to lay flat in the pan and cook evenly.

Place a dry nonstick frying pan over high heat and put in the chicken, skin side down. Fry until the skin is brown and crispy, pressing down on the chicken occasionally with a spatula. Turn the chicken over and cook until done—it's done when you poke the middle with a fork or knife tip and the juices run clear. Remove the chicken from the pan and wipe the pan clean with a paper towel.

Put the mirin, soy sauce, and sugar in the pan over medium-high heat, and stir until the sugar is melted. When the sauce is bubbling, return the chicken to the pan, and coat it with the sauce on both sides. Remove from the pan to a plate and let cool. Slice and pack. Sprinkle with shichimi pepper.

Pan-steamed Sweet Potato

1 SERVING

This method of cooking sweet potato really brings out its flavors. With such a simple dish, the quality of the ingredients really makes a difference, so use good sea salt and honey. You can leave on the skin of the potato for extra fiber and color, or peel it. I have used the white-fleshed, pink-skinned type of sweet potato that is common in Japan (look for these at Asian markets), but you could use the orange-skinned type or whatever variety you can buy locally.

½ small sweet potato, sliced into rounds ½ inch (1cm) thick
⅛ tsp sea salt
1 tsp honey, optional

Put the sweet potato slices into a pan in a single layer. Add just enough water to come up to half the height of the slices. Sprinkle with the sea salt.

Cover and cook over medium-low heat for about 8–10 minutes, turning once, until the potato slices are cooked through. Drain off any remaining water. For a sweeter flavor, drizzle the potato slices with honey while still in the pan, turning to coat. Let cool before packing.

Cucumber and Turnip Salad with Yuzu

4 SERVINGS

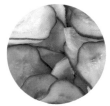

Yuzu is a tart, slightly bitter citrus fruit that is common in Japan. It's getting rather trendy around the world these days, used in everything from cosmetics to macarons. If you can't get hold of yuzu, use lime instead.

This refreshing, crunchy pickle-salad can be made in advance and stored in the refrigerator, so I've given amounts to make about 4 bento-sized servings.

1 medium English cucumber
2 small Japanese turnips, or ½ large Western turnip
1 tsp salt
½ tsp grated or dried yuzu peel, or lime peel
½ Tbsp fresh or bottled yuzu juice, or lime juice

Cut the cucumber in half lengthwise. If there are a lot of seeds inside, scoop them out with a spoon. Slice thinly, using a vegetable slicer, food processor, or mandoline.

Slice the turnips and cut the slices into pieces about the same size as the cucumber slices.

Massage the salt into the vegetables with your hands until the vegetables are limp. Squeeze well to expel excess moisture. Add the yuzu peel and juice and mix well. Let rest, covered, for a minimum of 20 minutes, overnight if possible.

Basic White Rice

1 SERVING

This bento is made with 1 cup (200g) cooked Basic White Rice (see page 53).

Have hot precooked rice ready to go. Either set the timer on your rice cooker the night before so that the rice is ready in the morning or defrost some pre-cooked frozen rice in the microwave (see page 118). See page 16 for how to make great-tasting bento rice, and page 17 for rice packing instructions.

Apple Bunnies

See page 75 for instructions. If you're in a hurry, just put in some plain apple wedges that have been dunked in cold water with salt or lemon juice added to prevent browning.

VARIATION RECIPES

Teriyaki

Did you know that bottled teriyaki sauce is a product that was created for the North American market? Ready-made teriyaki sauce is not widely sold in Japan, since it's easy to make with commonly available ingredients. The basic formula is to add soy sauce, mirin, saké, and a sweetener such as sugar or honey to the meat or fish juices in the pan.

Teriyaki recipes are great for bentos because the glaze keeps the meat or fish moist. Remember to cool the cooked items before packing.

Honey Salmon Teriyaki

1 SERVING

1 piece salted salmon (see page 39) 1 tsp mirin
1 tsp soy sauce   sansho or black pepper, to taste
1 tsp honey

Fry the salmon in a dry nonstick frying pan over medium-high heat for 3–4 minutes on each side

until just cooked, then remove from pan. Put the soy sauce, honey, and mirin in the pan and stir to combine. When the liquid is bubbling, return the salmon to the pan for 1–2 minutes, turning to coat it in the sauce. Sprinkle with sansho or black pepper.

Mackerel Teriyaki

1 SERVING

1 tsp vegetable oil
3 oz (90g) mackerel fillet, or other blue, oily fish, boned
2 Tbsp saké
1 tsp peeled and grated fresh ginger
1 Tbsp soy sauce
1 tsp sugar
pickled or fresh ginger, finely julienned, for garnish

Heat the oil in a nonstick frying pan over high heat. Put in the mackerel, skin side down, and fry for 4–5 minutes until the skin is browned, then turn over and cook for 2–3 minutes until done (the fish should look opaque rather than transparent when you pierce it in the middle). Remove the fish and wipe the pan clean with a paper towel. Put the saké, ginger, soy sauce, and sugar in the pan over medium heat. When the sauce is bubbling and slightly syrupy, add the fish back to the pan. Turn the fish to coat in the sauce. Sprinkle with the ginger after packing.

Prosciutto-wrapped Tofu Teriyaki

1 SERVING

This is also good without the sweet-salty sauce.

1 piece firm tofu, about 3 x 2 x 1 inch (8 x 5 x 2.5cm)
1 slice thin-cut prosciutto, or other salty cured ham, cut in half
1 tsp olive oil
1 tsp soy sauce
1 tsp mirin
1 tsp maple syrup
black pepper, to taste

Cut the tofu in half and lay on paper towels to absorb excess moisture. Wrap each tofu half in a slice of prosciutto.

Heat the olive oil in a nonstick frying pan over medium heat and fry the prosciutto-wrapped tofu slices until the prosciutto is crispy. Remove from the pan, and wipe the pan out with a paper towel.

Place the pan back over medium heat, put in the soy sauce, mirin, and maple syrup, and stir to combine. When the sauce is bubbling and slightly syrupy, return the prosciutto-wrapped tofu slices to the pan and turn to coat in the sauce. Sprinkle with a little black pepper.

Shiitake Teriyaki

1 SERVING

The teriyaki sauce makes shiitake mushrooms taste satisfyingly meaty.

vegetable oil, for sautéing
3 small fresh shiitake mushrooms, stems removed
1 Tbsp soy sauce
1 Tbsp mirin
1 tsp sugar
sansho pepper, to taste

Heat the oil in a frying pan over high heat, and sauté the shiitake for 5–6 minutes until browned and tender. Remove from the pan. Put the soy sauce, mirin, and sugar in the pan, turn the heat to medium, and stir to combine. When the sauce is bubbling, return the mushrooms to the pan and toss to coat in the sauce. Sprinkle with sansho pepper before packing.

Teriyaki Hamburger

1–2 SERVINGS

4 Mini-hamburgers, frozen (see page 27)
1 Tbsp soy sauce
1 Tbsp mirin
1 tsp peeled and grated fresh ginger
1 tsp sugar

Defrost the hamburgers following the instructions on page 27. Put all the other ingredients in a frying pan over medium heat and stir to combine. When the sauce is bubbling, put the hamburgers in the pan and turn a few times to coat in the sauce.

Teriyaki Ham

1 SERVING

This is a great way to use up leftover cooked ham. Adjust the amount of soy sauce according to how salty the ham is.

3 oz (90g) baked or boiled ham, sliced into bento-box-sized pieces
1 Tbsp soy sauce
2 Tbsp orange or pineapple juice
pinch ground allspice
1 tsp brown sugar
pinch sweet paprika

Heat up a dry nonstick frying pan and put in the ham. Fry over high heat for 1–2 minutes on each side until just lightly browned, and remove from the pan. Put the soy sauce, fruit juice, allspice, and sugar in the pan over medium heat and stir until slightly syrupy. Return the ham to the pan and turn in the sauce to coat. Sprinkle with the paprika.

TIMELINE

MINUTES	15	10	5	0
Rice (precooked)	☑ pack into bento box, let cool			
Chicken Kijiyaki	☑ heat up frying pan ☑ put chicken in, skin side down	☑ turn chicken over, cook 2–3 min	☑ add sauce, coat chicken, let cool	☑ pack into bento box on top of rice
Pan-steamed Sweet Potato	☑ slice potato, put into pan with water and salt	☑ take out and let cool		☑ pack into bento box
Cucumber and Turnip Salad with Yuzu				☑ pack into bento box
Apple Bunnies		☑ cut apple ☑ dunk into water with lemon juice		☑ pack into bento box

Make in advance: Cucumber and Turnip Salad.

Prep the night before: Set timer on rice cooker, if using. Pierce chicken on skin side.

Sukiyaki-style Beef Donburi Bento

A donburi is a meal in a bowl, consisting of rice with various savory toppings. Here the bento box is the bowl, and the topping is a savory-sweet mixture that is reminiscent of sukiyaki, the classic Japanese beef hotpot.

CONTENTS

- Quick Sukiyaki
- Simmered Carrot and Daikon
- Blanched Snow Peas
- Basic White Rice

BEEF NOTE: *You can find thinly sliced beef for making sukiyaki at Japanese grocery stores. If you can't find sukiyaki beef, you can use cheesesteak beef slices, or thinly slice a piece of well-marbled sirloin. (Putting the meat in the freezer for an hour beforehand makes slicing it thinly much easier.)*

DECORATION NOTE: *I've used a tiny edible chrysanthemum as a decorative accent. Edible flowers are a way to add instant visual appeal to your bentos.*

AHEAD-OF-TIME NOTE: *This can be made the night before. The flavors will deepen with rest.*

Quick Sukiyaki

1 SERVING

Sukiyaki is eaten at the table as it is cooked, but I always loved leftover sukiyaki the day after. This quick sukiyaki gives the cooked-in flavor of day-after sukiyaki without the wait.

1¾ oz (50g) enoki mushrooms
1 tsp vegetable oil
4 inch (10cm) piece of the white part of a leek, thinly sliced
1 fresh shiitake mushroom, sliced, stem discarded
3 oz (90g) sukiyaki ready beef
1 Tbsp sugar
¼ cup (60ml) dashi stock (see page 118)
2 Tbsp soy sauce
1 Tbsp mirin
1 Tbsp saké
shichimi pepper, to taste

Cut off the stuck-together roots of the enoki mushrooms and shred the mushrooms apart.

Heat the oil in a small frying pan over high heat. Put in the leek and sauté until limp. Add the enoki and shiitake and sauté for a further 3–4 minutes.

Add the beef and sugar and stir rapidly until the beef has started to brown. Add all the other ingredients. Cook rapidly over high heat for 3–4 minutes. Turn off the heat and transfer the contents of the pan to a bowl. When cool, put the mixture on top of the rice with some of the cooking liquid. Sprinkle with shichimi pepper.

Simmered Carrot and Daikon

1 SERVING

This simply flavored vegetable side is a nice contrast to the salty-sweet flavors of the beef.

½ medium carrot
2 inch (5cm) length daikon radish
1 cup (240ml) dashi stock (see page 118)
½ tsp salt

Peel and cut the carrot and daikon into slices or decorative shapes. Simmer in the dashi with the salt until just tender. Let the vegetables cool in the dashi, so that they absorb the flavor.

AHEAD-OF-TIME NOTE: *This can be made up to 3 days ahead and kept in the refrigerator.*

Blanched Snow Peas

1 SERVING

This is a simple, yet colorful and nutritious garnish.

handful snow peas, topped and tailed, strings removed

Cook in boiling water for a couple of minutes until crisp-tender. Drain and cool rapidly under running water. Arrange in a decorative pattern on top of the sukiyaki.

Basic White Rice

1 SERVING

This bento is made with 1 cup (200g) cooked Basic White Rice (see page 53).

Have hot precooked rice ready to go. Either set the timer on your rice cooker the night before so that the rice is ready in the morning or defrost some pre-cooked frozen rice in the microwave (see page 118). See page 16 for how to make great-tasting bento rice, and page 17 for rice packing instructions.

TIMELINE

The flavors of both Quick Sukiyaki and Simmered Carrot and Daikon improve after resting, so I recommend that you make both the night before. So for this bento, there is no timeline. All you need to do is to mound the sukiyaki on top of the rice and tuck in the vegetables. You may want to pack a spoon or fork with this bento, since the rice can get a bit soupy from the sukiyaki juices.

VARIATION RECIPES
Donburi Bentos

Donburi-type bentos, where everything is just piled on top of a bed of rice, are for people who love rice flavored with the juices of the food that's on top. Donburi can be assembled in minutes, so they are great for busy mornings. Try combining various leftovers for an impromptu donburi.

Chicken and Egg Donburi

1 SERVING

This dish is called *oyako-don* in Japanese, meaning "parent-and-child bowl." Which came first, the chicken or the egg?

½ small onion, thinly sliced
1 tsp oil
3 oz (90g) boneless, skinless chicken, cut into bite-sized pieces
handful mitsuba or flat leaf parsley
1 egg
2 Tbsp dashi stock (see page 118)
1 Tbsp soy sauce
1 Tbsp mirin
1 cup (200g) cooked Basic White Rice (see facing page)

In a frying pan, sauté the onion in the oil until the onion is limp. Add the chicken and sauté until cooked. Add the mitsuba or parsley. In a small bowl, beat the egg with the dashi, soy sauce, and mirin. Add the egg mixture to the pan. Cook until the egg is just about set. Mound on top of the rice.

Mushroom and Fried Tofu Donburi

1 SERVING

This is a satisfying and flavor-packed vegan donburi made with the deep-fried tofu known as *abura-age*. You can vary this by substituting tofu, seitan, or your favorite vegetarian protein for the abura-age. If you cannot get maitake mushrooms (also known as hen-of-the-woods), use whatever mushrooms you have available. Incidentally, I recommend using brown rice in vegetarian dishes for the extra boost of nutrients it provides.

1 tsp sesame oil
1 tsp vegetable oil
4 inch (10cm) length of the white part of a leek, thinly sliced
1 sheet abura-age deep-fried tofu, sliced into strips
2 fresh shiitake mushrooms, sliced, stems discarded
½ cup (35g) separated maitake mushrooms
1 cup (35g) shredded greens such as chard or bok choy
2 Tbsp soy sauce
2 Tbsp saké
1 cup (200g) cooked Basic Brown Rice (see facing page)
sansho or black pepper, to taste

Heat the sesame oil and vegetable oil in a nonstick frying pan over high heat. Put in the leek and stir-fry until limp. Add the abura-age strips and the mushrooms and stir-fry until the mushrooms are browned. Add the greens and stir-fry for a further minute. Add the soy sauce and saké and simmer briefly. Remove from the heat. When cool, mound on top of the rice. Sprinkle with sansho or black pepper.

TIP: *A donburi-type bento can look like a dog's dinner without some care. To perk up its appearance, add some fresh-looking garnishes such as chopped parsley or mitsuba, green onion, chives, blanched snow peas, or brightly colored beni shoga pickled ginger. Colorful cutouts work well too. Use a bento box with an airtight lid to avoid any leaking.*

How to Cook Rice

Japanese-style Basic White Rice

MAKES 4 CUPS (800G) COOKED RICE

Rice, the staple food of Japan, is of such importance in Japanese cuisine that the word for cooked rice—*gohan*—is synonymous with "meal," and most Japanese-style bentos are created around plain, steamed rice. In order to taste authentically Japanese (and be acceptable to your Japanese friends), rice must be prepared in a certain way. Don't skip any steps because it's "just plain old rice"!

2 cups (400g) Japanese-style medium-grain white rice
water for rinsing
2½ cups (600ml) water, for cooking

Rinse the rice rapidly under running water, draining the water away when it turns white. Scrub the rice gently by squeezing it and mixing it around with your hands—this is referred to as "polishing" the rice in Japan. Run more fresh water over the rice and rinse again. Repeat these steps until the water runs clear. Drain the rice into a fine-mesh sieve or colander, and leave to dry out for ten minutes.

Put the rice and the 2½ cups of water into a heavy-bottomed pot with a tight-fitting lid. Turn the heat to high and bring the water up to a boil. Immediately turn the heat to low, put on the lid, and leave to steam gently for 15–20 minutes, until the water has been absorbed—you should see small, even holes all over the surface of the rice. Turn the heat to high for a couple of minutes so that any remaining water evaporates.

Turn off the heat, and remove the lid. Drape a clean, dry kitchen towel over the pot and put the lid back on. Leave the pot to steam for 10–15 minutes. Don't be tempted to skip this step—it plumps up the rice grains and makes them really delicious.

Remove the lid and the towel, and fluff up the rice with a rice paddle.

If using a rice cooker, rinse the rice following the above instructions and cook the rice according to the manufacturer's instructions.

TIP: *For sushi rice, add a 4 inch (10cm) length of dried konbu seaweed or a teaspoon of instant dashi granules to the cooking water.*

Basic Brown Rice

MAKES 4 CUPS (800G) COOKED RICE

I've tried several methods of cooking brown rice, from using a pressure cooker to soaking the rice for a long time. This method, which I discovered recently and which originates in northern Japan, uses a regular cooking pot and doesn't require long soaking. It makes very plump, tender rice.

2 cups (400g) medium-grain brown rice
water for rinsing
½ tsp salt
3 cups water (720ml), for cooking
1½–2 cups (360–480ml) additional cold water

Rinse the brown rice in the same way as the white rice, until the water runs clear. (Brown rice needs less rinsing than white rice.) Drain into a fine-mesh sieve or colander and leave to dry out for 10 minutes.

Put the rice, salt, and the 3 cups of water into a heavy-bottomed pot with a tight-fitting lid, and turn the heat to high. Bring to a boil, and keep cooking over high heat for 10–15 minutes, until the water has evaporated and you start to hear the rice grains pop.

Add the 1½–2 cups of additional cold water to the pot (use less if you like your rice firm and chewy, more if you prefer softer rice), and stir the rice grains around. Adding cold water to the hot rice causes the hard hull of the rice grain to crack, so that the rice cooks faster. Bring the pot back up to a boil, then turn the heat to low and put the lid on. Cook for a further 10–15 minutes, until the water has been absorbed into the rice.

Turn off the heat, and remove the lid. Drape a clean, dry kitchen towel over the pot, and put the lid back on. Leave the pot to steam for 10–15 minutes. Don't be tempted to skip this step—it plumps up the rice grains and makes them really delicious.

Remove the lid and the towel, and fluff up the rice with a rice paddle.

If using a rice cooker with a "brown rice" setting, rinse the rice following the above instructions and cook according to the manufacturer's instructions.

Tofu Nugget Bento

This is a vegan bento that is satisfying even for non–meat eaters. It takes its inspiration from the Buddhist temple cuisine known as *shojin ryori*. Note that brown rice is used here instead of white, since a meatless bento can use the extra nutrition boost that brown rice provides.

CONTENTS

- Miso Tofu Nuggets with Edamame
- Sweet Pepper Kinpira
- Blanched Mizuna Greens with Ginger Sauce
- Basic Brown Rice with Umeboshi

Miso Tofu Nuggets with Edamame

3 SERVINGS (9 NUGGETS)

This is a denser, meatier version of *ganmodoki*, a classic deep-fried tofu dumpling that is supposed to mimic the flavor of *gan*—goose meat. I am not sure about that, but this is certainly tasty enough to satisfy even the most die-hard carnivore. Besides being vegan, it's gluten free.

3 Tbsp finely chopped green onion
2 tsp peeled and finely chopped fresh ginger
1 tsp sesame oil
3 Tbsp frozen or fresh shelled edamame beans
1 lb (450g) firm tofu, drained (see page 45 for how to drain)
3 Tbsp moromi miso, or miso of your choice
¼ tsp sea salt (omit if the miso you choose is salty)
cornstarch, for coating
vegetable oil, for deep-frying

Sauté the green onion and ginger in the sesame oil for a couple of minutes, then remove from the heat. Boil the edamame in just enough water to cover for about 5 minutes, until tender yet still firm. Alternatively, put the edamame on a plate, cover with plastic wrap, and microwave on high for 30 seconds.

Crumble the tofu in a bowl. Add the sautéed green onion and ginger, miso, and salt. Mix together thoroughly using your impeccably clean hands. Alternatively, you can mix this in a food processor, pulsing to combine. When everything is combined to a smooth paste, mix in the edamame.

Divide the tofu mixture into nine portions and form round- or oval-shaped flattened nuggets. Coat in cornstarch.

Heat 1 inch (2.5cm) of the oil in a large frying pan over medium-high heat. The oil is hot enough when a small piece of the cornstarch-coated tofu dropped into the oil turns brown in a few seconds. Fry the nuggets in batches, taking care not to overcrowd the pan, until browned on both sides. Drain well and cool before packing.

These nuggets can be frozen quite successfully. The texture will change a little, but they will still be good. Cold nuggets can be pan-fried in a dry nonstick frying pan over medium heat until crispy on the outside and heated through, or gently poached in dashi stock for a softer texture. They are also good in soup.

Sweet Pepper Kinpira

1 SERVING

Kinpira refers to a method of stir-frying shredded or julienned vegetables quickly in a fragrant, spicy oil. The vegetables stay crisp-tender. Kinpira tastes good hot or cold and is ideal for bentos. This sweet-pepper version provides a nice texture contrast to the rice and the tofu nuggets, as well as adding a bright splash of color.

2 tsp sesame oil
½ each yellow and red sweet pepper, de-seeded and sliced
1 Tbsp white sesame seeds, toasted
1 Tbsp soy sauce
pinch red chili flakes

Heat the oil in a frying pan over high heat and add the sweet peppers. Sauté for 3–4 minutes until they turn a brighter color but are still crisp. Add the sesame seeds, soy sauce, and chili. Stir until the soy sauce has evaporated. Let cool before packing.

AHEAD-OF-TIME NOTE: *Make this kinpira using two whole sweet peppers and doubling the other ingredients. It will keep for up to a week in the refrigerator.*

Blanched Mizuna Greens with Ginger Sauce

1 SERVING

The peppery flavor of the mizuna greens is enhanced by the ginger flavor. Try blanched arugula for an interesting alternative.

2 oz (60g) mizuna greens, washed and trimmed
juice from 1 tsp peeled and grated fresh ginger
2 tsp soy sauce
pinch bonito flakes

Bring a pan of water to the boil (using an electric kettle to boil the water speeds things up a lot). Put the mizuna in the pan and boil for a minute. Drain, and run cold water into the pan to cool the cooked mizuna rapidly. Drain again, and squeeze out as much moisture as possible.

If necessary, cut into shorter lengths that fit your bento divider cup. Add the ginger juice and soy sauce and mix well. Sprinkle with bonito flakes.

Basic Brown Rice with Umeboshi

1 SERVING

Have hot precooked rice ready to go. Either set the timer on your rice cooker the night before so that the rice is ready in the morning or defrost some precooked frozen rice in the microwave (see page 118). See page 16 for how to make great-tasting bento rice, and page 17 for rice packing instructions.

Since brown rice can spoil faster than white, I often like to pack it with an umeboshi plum. Umeboshi has antimicrobial qualities that help keep the rice fresh longer.

1 cup (200g) cooked Basic Brown Rice (see page 53)
1 umeboshi plum

Pack the rice into the bento box and place the umeboshi on top.

TIMELINE

I'm assuming you'll be making everything in the morning, but do remember that the tofu nuggets and kinpira and even the mizuna can be made in advance, leaving you to just assemble the bento quickly in the morning.

MINUTES	20	15	10	5	0
Rice (precooked)	☑ pack into bento box with umeboshi, let cool				
Miso Tofu Nuggets with Edamame	☑ sauté green onions and ginger	☑ heat up oil ☑ mix tofu, etc. together well	☑ fry nuggets ☑ form tofu nuggets	☑ take out and let cool ☑ pack into bento box	
Sweet Pepper Kinpira			☑ sauté peppers	☑ pack into bento box ☑ take out and let cool	
Blanched Mizuna Greens with Ginger Sauce		☑ blanch mizuna greens	☑ drain and let cool, squeeze out	☑ season	☑ pack into bento box

Prep the night before: Set timer or rice cooker, if using.
Chop and slice vegetables.
Drain tofu.
Cook edamame.

VARIATION RECIPES

Kinpira

Kinpira can be made with all kinds of firm vegetables such as peeled broccoli stems, shredded cabbage (the often-discarded stems are great for this), parsnips, or salsify. All kinpiras will keep for a week in the refrigerator and can also be frozen quite successfully.

Classic Kinpira Gobo

4–6 SERVINGS

This is the most classic kinpira, made just with burdock root—known as *gobo* in Japanese—a very crunchy vegetable that is popular throughout Asia.

1 burdock root
1 Tbsp vegetable oil
2 tsp sesame oil
½ cup (120ml) dashi stock (see page 118)
1 Tbsp sugar
3 Tbsp soy sauce
2 Tbsp white sesame seeds, toasted
shichimi pepper, to taste

Peel the burdock root (cutting it into sections first helps) and cut into thin slices on the diagonal. Cut the slices into matchsticks. Put the matchsticks into a bowl of water and leave for 15 minutes.

Heat the oil in a frying pan or wok over high heat. Put in the well-drained burdock and stir-fry briefly. Add the dashi, sugar, and soy sauce and cook rapidly until the liquid has evaporated. Add the sesame seeds and stir until they pop. Sprinkle with shichimi pepper to taste.

Carrot and Gobo Kinpira

This is as traditional as all-burdock kinpira, and is often also called kinpira gobo. Follow the above recipe, substituting half the burdock root for carrot, cut into the same size matchsticks as the burdock. You can omit the sugar if you prefer, since carrot has an inherent sweetness. This is my favorite kind of kinpira. Kinpira made just with carrot is also very good.

Salt and Pepper Celery Kinpira

4–6 SERVINGS

To my mind, celery is about as Western a vegetable as there is. Nevertheless, it makes great kinpira.

2 celery stalks
1 Tbsp good olive oil
½ tsp salt
plenty of black pepper, for seasoning
soy sauce, for drizzling, optional

Slice the celery thinly on the diagonal. Heat the olive oil in a frying pan or wok over high heat and put in the celery. Sauté until crisp-tender. Add the salt and plenty of black pepper. Drizzle with a tiny bit of soy sauce if you like.

Fennel Kinpira

4–6 SERVINGS

Fennel is another very "Western" vegetable that is great as kinpira.

1 Tbsp good olive oil
1 large fennel bulb, very thinly sliced
½ tsp salt
1 tsp Worcestershire sauce
1 tsp anise seeds
pinch red chili flakes

Heat the olive oil in a frying pan or wok over high heat and put in the fennel. Sauté until crisp-tender. Add the salt, Worcestershire sauce, and anise seeds. Add chili flakes to taste.

Hard Parts of a Cabbage Kinpira

4–6 SERVINGS

The tough, thick veins and the core of the cabbage—the parts that you might usually throw away—are used here, making this is a very economical dish. The tiny bit of sugar counteracts any bitter flavor.

1 tsp vegetable oil
thick veins and core of one large cabbage, cut into small matchsticks
1 tsp sesame oil
¼ tsp salt
1 tsp sugar
1 Tbsp balsamic vinegar
1 Tbsp soy sauce
pinch red chili flakes

Heat the vegetable oil in a frying pan or wok and add the cabbage. Sauté until crisp-tender. Add the sesame oil, salt, sugar, and balsamic vinegar. Stir to combine. Push the cabbage mixture to one side of the pan and add the soy sauce to the hot surface of the pan so that it sizzles. Stir rapidly to combine with the cabbage. Add red chili flakes to taste.

VARIATION: *Use peeled broccoli stalks instead of the cabbage, and omit the balsamic vinegar.*

Soba Noodle Bento

Soba noodles provide a nice change of pace from rice-based bentos. The accompaniments are a simple hard-boiled egg and a cold crabmeat salad. Served chilled, this bento is a great lunch for a hot summer's day.

CONTENTS

Cold Soba Noodles

1 SERVING

Rinsing the cooked noodles in cold water after boiling them may seem strange if you're used to Italian pasta and other Western noodles, but it's a necessary process for any Japanese dried noodles. It gets rid of the excess surface starch, prevents the noodles from sticking together, and gives the noodles a nice firm texture. Dried soba noodles usually come packaged in single-portion bundles of 100 grams (3½ ounces) each. If the soba you have isn't bundled, either see how many grams are in the package and divide accordingly, or weigh out a portion.

For the noodles
3½ oz (100g) dried soba noodles

For the condiments
2 Tbsp finely chopped green onion
½ Tbsp white sesame seeds, toasted
1 Tbsp finely shredded nori seaweed
shichimi pepper, to taste

Bring a large pot of water to a boil—soba noodles need plenty of water to cook. Using an electric kettle to boil the water will speed things up.

Put the noodles in the boiling water and lower the heat. The water should just bubble gently, not be at a rolling boil as for Italian pasta. Stir gently with chopsticks until the noodles are immersed in the water. Cook for 5–8 minutes, until the noodles are cooked through—they should be softer than Italian pasta, with no uncooked core, a bit past the al dente stage. If the water threatens to foam out of the pan as the noodles cook, add a little cold water.

Drain the noodles into a colander to get rid of the boiling water. Fill the pot with cold water, and put the noodles back in to cool them down rapidly. Rinse the soba noodles for about 5 minutes, rubbing the noodles gently with your hands and changing the water frequently or just letting water run from the tap, until they feel smooth and firm and not at all sticky.

Take little bundles of a few strands of soba at a time out of the water, and drain them on a flat basket or in a colander.

AHEAD-OF-TIME NOTE: *You can cook the noodles the night before and store them in the refrigerator, though they will become a little limp. Make sure you store them well covered, since cooked soba absorbs any refrigerator odors like a sponge.*

CONDIMENT VARIATIONS: *Two traditionally Japanese condiments for cold noodles are finely shredded green shiso leaves, and finely sliced myoga (the flower buds of a type of ginger). If you can get hold of either one of these, they will add a wonderful flavor to the soba.*

Dipping Sauce

MAKES ½ CUP (120ML)

¼ cup (60ml) dashi stock (see page 118)
¼ cup (60ml) kaeshi (see below)

Combine the dashi and the kaeshi. Alternatively, use store-bought ready-made noodle-sauce concentrate, called *men-tsuyu* (available in the bottled sauce section of a Japanese grocery store), diluted according the instructions on the bottle (usually a 50/50 mix of water and men-tsuyu).

Pack the dipping sauce in a separate container that closes very securely—I like to use a small jam jar with a screw-top lid. To eat, just pour the sauce over the soba, add the condiments, and mix well. You can have the egg separately, or mash it into the noodles and sauce—delicious!

Kaeshi

MAKES 6 CUPS (1.4L)

Kaeshi is a Japanese noodle soup concentrate. If you like Japanese noodles, you may want to keep a bottle of this concentrate on hand. All you need to do to make delicious noodle soup is mix it with some dashi stock. Kaeshi can also be used in any recipe that calls for soy sauce, mirin, and sugar.

This recipe makes 6 cups (1.4L), which lasts a long time, but you can halve or even quarter the quantities.

¾ cup (180ml) mirin
¾ cup (150g) granulated or superfine white sugar
4¼ cups (1L) dark soy sauce

Put the mirin in a saucepan over high heat and bring to a boil. Lower the heat and simmer for 5–6 minutes.

Add the sugar and stir until melted. Add the soy sauce and heat up slowly over medium-low heat, stirring several times, until the surface is barely bubbling. It should not boil vigorously or the flavor of the soy sauce will dissipate. Simmer gently for 5 minutes, skimming off any white scum that forms on the surface.

Let cool and store in a glass jar or other nonreactive, airtight container. The kaeshi can be used immediately but is better if rested for at least a day. Store in the refrigerator or other cool, dark place. It will keep for several months.

Crabmeat and Cabbage Salad

1 SERVING

This crunchy salad could be described as a crabmeat slaw. Use canned crabmeat, imitation crabsticks, or dressed crab from the fish counter. You can add some shredded carrot if you like.

1 cup (70g) finely shredded cabbage
¼ tsp salt
1 Tbsp rice vinegar
1 tsp sugar
¼ cup (30g) crabmeat
sansho or black pepper, to taste

Massage the shredded cabbage with the salt until the cabbage has wilted—it will shrink down in mass quite a bit. Squeeze well to expel excess moisture. Put in a bowl, add the vinegar and sugar, and mix. Add the crabmeat and taste; add a little more salt if needed. Sprinkle with sansho or black pepper.

PACKING TIP: *This is one of the few bentos that should be packed with an ice pack—not necessarily for safety, but just because cold soba noodles taste better when chilled.*

Hard-boiled Egg

Select eggs that are not freshly laid—supermarket eggs are fine. Put in a pan and add cold water to cover. Bring to a boil while rolling the eggs around occasionally to stop the yolk from settling to one side. Once the water is boiling, turn off the heat and place a lid on the pan. Leave for 10 minutes.

Drain, and run cold water over the eggs until they are completely cooled. Crack the shells all over and peel immersed in water, making sure any small bits of shell are washed off. Unpeeled eggs can be stored in the refrigerator for 3–4 days; peeled eggs for 1–2 days.

VARIATION RECIPES
Cold Noodle Dishes

For these cold noodle bento variations, use two bento boxes or a two-compartment bento box—one for the noodles, and one for the salad ingredients. I recommend carrying an ice pack to keep the noodles cool until lunchtime.

Somen Noodle Salad with Sesame Dressing

1 SERVING

Somen is a thin wheat noodle, rather like angel-hair pasta, that cooks in just a few minutes. It's usually served cold as part of a refreshing summer meal. It makes a great base for a noodle salad.

For the noodles
3½ oz (100g) dried somen noodles

For the salad
½ medium carrot, finely shredded
½ cup (50g) bean sprouts, roots trimmed, blanched in boiling water

1 green onion, finely shredded
2 oz (60g) roast pork or ham, finely shredded
2–3 shiso leaves or 2–3 watercress sprigs, shredded

For the dressing
2 Tbsp dashi stock (see page 118)
2 Tbsp kaeshi (see page 59)
2 Tbsp tahini or sesame paste

1 Tbsp rice vinegar
1 Tbsp sesame seeds, toasted
shichimi pepper, to taste

Cook the somen noodles using the same method as for soba noodles (see page 59), but reduce the cooking time to 3–4 minutes. Drain and rinse the noodles well, then strain them in a colander. Arrange the somen noodles in little bundles in your bento box.

Put the salad ingredients in a separate container or second bento box. Combine the dressing ingredients and carry in a separate, leakproof container. Pack the shichimi pepper in its own container, or in a folded piece of aluminum foil.

To eat, arrange the salad ingredients on top of the noodles. Pour the dressing over everything and sprinkle with shichimi pepper. Mix well and enjoy.

Cold Udon Noodles with Miso-peanut Meat Sauce

1 SERVING

Udon is a thick, chewy wheat noodle. There are two kinds of udon—the fresh type, which is sold frozen or refrigerated in Japanese grocery stores; and the dried type. Here I have used the dried type, which tends to hold up better when kept for a few hours before eating. The Miso-peanut Meat Sauce can be used in many kinds of dishes.

3½ oz (100g) dried udon noodles
½ cup (120g) Miso-peanut Meat Sauce (see this page)
1 cup (100g) bean sprouts, roots trimmed
⅓ English cucumber, de-seeded and sliced thinly
3–4 red radishes, thinly sliced
1 green onion, finely chopped

Cook the udon noodles using the same method as for soba noodles (see page 59), but increase the cooking time to 8–10 minutes. Drain and rinse the noodles well, then strain them in a colander. Arrange the udon noodles in the bento box.

Bring some water up to a boil in a small pan. Add the bean sprouts and boil for 1 minute. Drain, and refresh under cold running water. Drain well.

Pack the vegetables in a separate container or second bento box. Pack the Miso-peanut Meat Sauce into a bento divider cup. To eat, put the vegetables and the meat sauce on top of the noodles. Mix well and enjoy.

Miso-peanut Meat Sauce

MAKES 4 CUPS (1L)

This is a rich, very flavorful sauce that can be used for noodles or rice, or as a dipping sauce for raw vegetables. It keeps in the refrigerator for a week and can be frozen for up to 3 months.

12 oz (340g) red or Hatcho miso
4 Tbsp saké
2 Tbsp mirin
5 Tbsp sugar
½ cup (120ml) dashi stock (see page 118) or water
14 oz (400g) ground beef
1 Tbsp peeled and finely chopped fresh ginger
3 Tbsp finely chopped green onion
1 Tbsp vegetable oil
1 Tbsp sesame oil
2 Tbsp roughly chopped peanuts, raw or dry-roasted

Combine the miso, saké, mirin, sugar, and dashi stock or water to form a smooth paste. Set aside.

In a frying pan or wok, sauté the ground beef, ginger, and onion in the vegetable oil over high heat until the meat is browned. Drain off any excess fat. Add the sesame oil and peanuts. Add the miso mixture and turn the heat to medium-low. Cook, stirring frequently, until the sauce is thick and glossy. Let cool completely before storing in the refrigerator.

To make this spicy, add 1 teaspoon red chili flakes (or more if you like) after the beef has browned.

TIMELINE

MINUTES	15	10	5	0
Cold Soba Noodles	☑ boil water in electric kettle ☑ cook soba		☑ drain and rinse	☑ pack into bento box
Dipping Sauce and Condiments	☑ mix sauce together ☑ prepare condiments			☑ pack into bento box
Crabmeat and Cabbage Salad			☑ pack into bento box	
Hard-boiled Egg			☑ peel and cut	☑ pack into bento box with cherry tomatoes

Prep the night before: Boil egg (make extra for later meals). Crabmeat and Cabbage Salad.

Onigiri and Meatball Bento

Onigiri—rice balls—are an integral part of Japanese culture. They've even been described as Japanese soul food. They are portable, filling, and somehow very comforting. Here, they are paired with simple yet equally satisfying shrimp-and-pork meatballs.

CONTENTS

- Sweet and Sour Shrimp and Pork Balls
- Orange Carrots
- Blanched Asparagus Tips
- Plain Salted Onigiri

Sweet and Sour Shrimp and Pork Balls

3–4 SERVINGS (12 MEATBALLS)

These meatballs can be steam-cooked in the microwave in no time.

For the meatballs

3½ oz (100g) peeled shrimps, roughly chopped
7 oz (200g) ground pork
3 Tbsp finely chopped onion
1 tsp peeled and grated fresh ginger
1 Tbsp saké
1 Tbsp soy sauce
2 Tbsp cornstarch
½ tsp salt
2 Tbsp frozen mixed vegetables
1 Tbsp vegetable oil

For the sauce

1 Tbsp cornstarch
2 Tbsp water
½ cup (120ml) chicken stock
2 Tbsp rice vinegar
1 Tbsp soy sauce
1 Tbsp sugar

With your hands, mix all the meatball ingredients thoroughly except for the mixed vegetables and the oil, until the meat gets slightly sticky. Add the mixed vegetables last. Form the mixture into balls.

Place the meatballs in a circle on a microwave-safe plate and drizzle with the oil, turning them so that they are coated. Loosely cover the plate with plastic wrap. Microwave on high for 3 minutes.

If you don't have a microwave, steam the meatballs for 8–10 minutes in a steamer lined with kitchen parchment paper.

While the meatballs cook, make the sauce. Combine all the sauce ingredients in a small pan and mix. When the cornstarch has dissolved, place the pan over high heat and cook while stirring. When the sauce has thickened and looks clear rather than cloudy, add the still-hot meatballs and toss to coat with the sauce. Cool before packing.

AHEAD-OF-TIME NOTE: *You can freeze the uncooked meatballs lined up individually on a plate or baking sheet. Once frozen, pack into freezer bags or containers. Frozen meatballs will need to be microwaved for 4 minutes or longer. Cooked meatballs will keep in the refrigerator for 2–3 days. If I'm making meatballs for dinner, I set aside a few for the next day's bento. Cooked meatballs can be also be frozen; let cool to room temperature before packing into freezer containers or plastic bags. Reheat in the microwave for 5–6 minutes per 3–4 meatballs. I recommend freezing the "dry" meatballs separately from the sauce. You can vary them by combining them with other flavors, such as tomato sauce, sriracha sauce, or ketchup.*

Orange Carrots

4 SERVINGS

Orange-colored carrots are cooked in freshly squeezed orange juice—a double-orange recipe! This sweet-savory vegetable dish is perfect for bentos.

juice and peel of 1 medium organic or untreated orange
2 medium carrots, sliced or cut into decorative shapes
2 tsp sugar
pinch salt

Take a strip of peel from the orange with a sharp knife or vegetable peeler. Make sure there is no white pith on the orange peel, otherwise the carrots will turn bitter.

Place the carrot slices in a saucepan with the orange juice, peel, sugar, and salt. Add just enough water to completely submerge the carrots. Cook over high heat for 5–6 minutes until tender. Remove the peel. Drain the carrots before packing into a bento box.

AHEAD-OF-TIME NOTE: *These carrots can be made up to a week in advance and stored in the refrigerator. Keep the slices submerged in the cooking liquid and well covered. They can be frozen, but will turn a bit soft.*

Blanched Asparagus Tips

1 SERVING

2 cups (480ml) water
pinch salt
4–5 medium asparagus tips, 4 inches (10cm) long or to fit your bento box

Bring the 2 cups of water to a boil in a small pan. (Boiling the water in an electric kettle speeds up this process.) Add the salt and asparagus to the pan. Boil for 4–5 minutes, until crisp-tender. Drain off the boiling water, and run cold water over the asparagus to fix the color. Drain well before packing into a bento box.

1

Plain Salted Onigiri

1 SERVING (2 RICE BALLS)

Onigiri are often made with fillings in the center, but this recipe is for the most basic kind of onigiri: a ball of salted rice wrapped in nori seaweed. Two methods of making onigiri are listed below. Whichever you use, make sure that the rice is hot or very warm so that it sticks together properly.

2

½ tsp finely ground sea salt
1½ cups (300g) cooked Basic White Rice (see page 53), hot
2 strips nori seaweed, 6 x 1 inches (15 x 2.5cm)

Toast the nori, before or after cutting into strips, by laying it flat for no more than a few seconds on a heated griddle or dry frying pan. Set aside.

3

Making onigiri using plastic wrap

This method is easy for beginners and keeps your hands from getting covered with rice.

Using a spoon or rice paddle, lightly mix the salt into the hot cooked rice in the pan or rice cooker bowl.
    Line a small cup or bowl with plastic wrap (1).
    Divide the rice into 2 portions. Put 1 portion of rice into the plastic wrap–lined cup or bowl (2).
    Gather the ends of the plastic wrap around the rice and twist them tight (3).
     Form the rice ball by pressing over the plastic with your hands into a round, a triangle, or any shape you prefer. A triangle is the classic shape (4).
    Remove the rice from the plastic. Repeat with the remaining rice.
    Wrap each onigiri with a strip of nori seaweed (6). Or if you prefer, carry the nori seaweed strip separately, and wrap it around the onigiri just before eating. This will keep the nori crisper.

4

5

Making onigiri using the bare hands method

Moisten your palms with water and shake off the excess. Smear the ½ teaspoon of salt onto your palms.

Divide the rice into 2 portions. Put 1 portion of rice onto your palm (1)—be careful, the rice is hot!

Gently start to compress the rice into shape as you turn it in your hands. The shape can be a triangle, a round, a cylinder, or anything you like (2–4).

1   2

3   4

Different Types of Onigiri

The easiest type of onigiri to make yourself is the plain rice onigiri shown on these pages. You can mix the rice with flavorings such as chopped pickles, soboro, or furikake.

The most common type of onigiri in shops or restaurants has a small quantity of savory filling in the middle, and is usually wrapped with nori seaweed. Some popular fillings include canned tuna mixed with mayonnaise; an umeboshi plum; grilled salted salmon; bonito flakes moistened with soy sauce; or grilled salted fish roe. Be creative—try a tiny meatball, cooked shrimp, shredded barbecued beef, or whatever strikes your fancy. Make sure the filling is not too watery or oily, or the rice may fall apart.

Onigiri can also be formed like sushi, with extra ingredients on top, often held in place with a band of nori seaweed. Spam musubi is a Hawaiian speciality that consists of a crispy piece of fried Spam on top of a rice ball.

Onigiri can be formed into any shape. Traditional shapes include triangle, flattened circle, ball, and cylinder. Onigiri can also be decorated on the surface in all kinds of ways. A cute decorated onigiri is often the centerpiece of a bento.

TIMELINE

This timeline assumes that you make the meatballs and the carrots ahead of time.
Onigiri are really best when made in the morning, using freshly cooked hot rice.

MINUTES	15	10	5	0
Onigiri (with precooked rice)		☑ make onigiri	☑ let cool	☑ pack into bento box
Sweet and Sour Shrimp and Pork Balls	☑ heat meatballs and sauce through, or defrost	☑ let cool		☑ pack into bento box
Orange Carrots				☑ pack into bento box
Blanched Asparagus Tips	☑ boil water / ☑ blanch asparagus	☑ let cool		☑ pack into bento box

Make in advance: Sweet and Sour Shrimp and Pork Balls.

Prep the night before: Set timer on rice cooker, if using.
Orange Carrots.
Cut nori.

Egg-wrapped Sushi Bento

Sushi does not have to be made with raw fish, which would not be suitable for a bento box that is to be eaten some hours after it's made. This is a homey sushi, made by wrapping a thin egg crepe around sushi rice.

CONTENTS

Egg-wrapped Sushi

1 SERVING (2 PIECES OF SUSHI)

The difference between onigiri and sushi is the rice. If something is called sushi, it means it's made with vinegar-flavored rice. Nigiri-zushi, the kind you see at sushi restaurants around the world, consisting of a piece of raw fish or something else on top of sushi rice, is just one kind of sushi. Simpler and more economical versions of sushi, such as this one, are enjoyed at home in Japan. Since no raw fish is involved, this is perfect for bentos.

This recipe teaches you two basics of Japanese cooking: how to make sushi rice, and how to make the very thin egg crepes known as *usuyaki tamago* in Japan. These egg crepes are used frequently in Japanese cooking, either whole as a wrapping—just as crepes made from flour are used—or thinly shredded. The shredded form is known as *kinshi tamago*—kinshi means "precious thread," and its bright yellow color is supposed to suggest the precious threads used for festive kimonos. Shredded egg is used in chirashi-zushi, a type of sushi where toppings are scattered over a bowl of sushi rice. It is also used as a garnish on cold noodles: try it as an alternative to the boiled egg for the Soba Noodle Bento on page 59.

In this recipe the crepe is used whole, as a wrapping. Some people make the crepe so thinly that you can read through it, but here I have made it on the thick side so that it is easier to handle. The cornstarch makes the crepe less likely to tear.

For the sushi rice

1½ cups (300g) Basic White Rice cooked with konbu seaweed or instant dashi granules (see page 53), hot

1–1½ Tbsp Sushi Vinegar (see page 119)

1 Tbsp white sesame seeds, toasted, optional

Combine the hot rice and the sushi vinegar in a large bowl. Mix rapidly with a spoon or rice spatula. Taste and add a little more sushi vinegar if you think it's needed. Let cool.

This is basic sushi rice. Hot rice must be used, otherwise the sushi vinegar will not be properly absorbed. When making a quantity of sushi rice, you or a handy assistant can fan the rice (or use the cold setting on a hair dryer) to cool it rapidly as you mix it. This will allow the rice to absorb the flavor of the vinegar while causing any excess moisture to evaporate, leaving the rice grains glossy and firm. Ideally, use an uncoated wooden bowl called a *hangiri* (the uncoated wood also absorbs excess moisture from the rice), but any bowl that is big enough to freely mix the rice will do, as long as you fan and cool the rice properly.

Toasted sesame seeds can be mixed into the sushi rice for added flavor and texture.

For the egg crepes

2 small eggs	2 tsp cornstarch
2 tsp sugar	vegetable oil, for frying
1 tsp saké or water	beni shoga pickled ginger, for
¼ tsp salt	garnish, optional

Mix all the ingredients together well with a fork or chopsticks, not a whisk—the mixture shouldn't be foamy—until the cornstarch has dissolved.

Strain the beaten egg mixture through a tea strainer or fine-mesh colander. This ensures that the crepe will be evenly colored throughout, with no white bits.

Make ready a folded, moistened kitchen towel and a wadded piece of paper towel.

Pour a little vegetable oil into an 8 inch (20cm) diameter nonstick frying pan over low heat, and spread the oil around the pan with the wadded paper towel (1, overleaf).

When the pan is hot, remove from the heat and press the bottom for a second on the moistened kitchen towel. This distributes the heat evenly across the base of the pan.

Place the pan back over low heat, pour in half the egg mixture, and let it cook (2, overleaf). If any large bubbles rise up, pierce them with a chopstick, and put the pan back on the moistened kitchen towel for a second to cool it down and even out the heat again.

When the egg is set, carefully lift it up with a spatula or chopstick and flip it over (3, overleaf). This does take some practice! (Alternatively, have a second hot, oiled frying pan ready, and flip the crepe into it.)

Cook the other side for a minute, then turn the crepe out onto a plate (4, overleaf).

Repeat the process with remaining egg mixture.

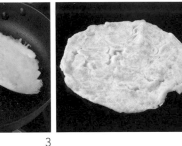

1 2 3 4

Slice the cucumber very thinly. Sprinkle with the salt and massage well with your hands until the cucumber is limp. Squeeze out the excess moisture.

Cover the wakame in cold water and soak for about 5 minutes until reconstituted.

In a small bowl, combine the lemon juice, olive oil, black pepper, and sugar with the cucumber. Mix in the smoked salmon.

AHEAD-OF-TIME NOTE: *This can be made the night before.*

When the crepes have cooled, divide the sushi rice in half and form 2 oval shapes. Wrap each with a crepe. Put in a bento box so that the smooth side of the egg-wrapped sushi faces upwards, and score the top of each piece of sushi in a crisscross pattern to show the inside. Decorate with a little beni shoga, a few carrot cutouts, or other colorful garnish.

AHEAD-OF-TIME NOTE: *The egg crepes can be made the night before and stored in the refrigerator. They also freeze well, stacked flat with a sheet of kitchen parchment paper between each crepe.*

HELP! MY CREPE'S RIPPED! *If your crepes don't turn out well, just shred them finely to use as a garnish. I often find that the first crepe tends to go awry—it ends up in my mouth as a cook's treat more often than not.*

Smoked Salmon, Wakame, and Cucumber Salad

1 SERVING

Since the egg-wrapped sushi takes some effort, this is an easy-to-assemble salad.

4 inch (10cm) length English cucumber
1 tsp dried wakame seaweed
pinch salt
1 tsp lemon juice
½ tsp olive oil
black pepper, to taste
pinch sugar
1 oz (30g) smoked salmon, shredded

Lotus Root Stewed with Hijiki Seaweed

4–6 SERVINGS

This dish is crunchy and full of fiber. You can find fresh or precooked lotus root at Asian or Chinese supermarkets. Hijiki seaweed is available at Japanese grocery stores. This keeps well in the refrigerator or the freezer, so it makes sense to make enough for several bentos.

3 Tbsp dried hijiki seaweed
1 fresh lotus root, about 9 inches (23cm) long
splash vinegar
½ Tbsp vegetable oil
1 tsp sesame oil
2 cups (480ml) dashi stock (see page 118)
2 Tbsp soy sauce
1 Tbsp mirin

Soak the hijiki seaweed in water for about 10 minutes until softened. Drain.

Peel and slice the lotus root. Dunk into cold water with a splash of vinegar to prevent it from turning black.

Heat the vegetable oil and sesame oil in a frying pan or wok over high heat. Put in the lotus root slices and stir-fry for 3–4 minutes. Add the other ingredients. Bring to a boil, then turn the heat to medium-low and simmer for 15–20 minutes.

AHEAD-OF-TIME NOTE: *This keeps in the refrigerator for a week, or in the freezer for a month.*

Inari-zushi

3 SERVINGS (6 PIECES OF INARI-ZUSHI)

Inari-zushi is sushi rice stuffed into pockets of deep-fried tofu that have been poached in a sweet-salty sauce. The pockets are made from the ready-made deep-fried tofu sheets called *abura-age* that can be found in Japanese grocery stores.

3 sheets abura-age deep-fried tofu
1½ cups (360ml) dashi stock (see page 118)
4 Tbsp sugar
2 Tbsp saké
2 Tbsp mirin
4 Tbsp soy sauce
3 cups (600g) prepared sushi rice (see page 67)
gari pickled ginger, for garnish, optional

Blanch the deep-fried tofu sheets in boiling water for a minute. This gets rid of excess oil and makes it easier to open them up to make pockets. Drain in a colander and leave to cool. When they are cool, cut each slice in half. You'll find that you can easily open up a pocket in each half.

Combine the dashi stock, sugar, saké, mirin, and soy sauce in a pan and bring to a boil. Put the tofu pockets in the pan, lower the heat to a simmer, and poach for 15 minutes. If you have the time, let the tofu cool in the seasoning liquid so that it absorbs more flavor.

Remove the tofu pockets from the pan and squeeze out the excess liquid. Stuff the pockets loosely with sushi rice—do not overstuff, or the skins may rip. Fold down the opening, and pack into the bento box with the folded side down. Garnish with gari.

AHEAD-OF-TIME NOTE: *The pockets can be made up to a couple of days in advance. Store them in the refrigerator, immersed in the seasoning liquid and well covered. You can also freeze the poached pockets for up to a month.*

INARI-ZUSHI TIPS: *You can add various ingredients to the sushi rice for added flavor. Toasted sesame seeds, finely chopped cooked vegetables, and even soboro (see page 43) all work well. Leftovers of Lotus Root Stewed with Hijiki Seaweed (see facing page), finely chopped, make a nice, crunchy addition. Add about 1 tablespoon of the extra ingredient per cup of rice.*

Prepackaged (canned or refrigerated) ready-poached and seasoned inari-zushi pockets are sometimes easier to find in Asian supermarkets in the West than plain abura-age. They are very convenient to use, though they are often more strongly flavored than I prefer. All you have to do before using is drain off the excess sauce they come packed in, then stuff with the sushi rice. These prepackaged pockets, especially the canned ones, tend to be very thin and delicate, so handle them carefully.

TIMELINE

This timeline is based on the assumption that you will make the egg crepes and the two side dishes the night before. The sushi rice tastes better if you prepare it in the morning.

MINUTES	10	5	0
Egg-wrapped Sushi	☑ mix sushi vinegar into warm rice, until cool	☑ make Egg-wrapped Sushi	☑ pack into bento box
Smoked Salmon, Wakame, and Cucumber Salad			☑ pack into bento box
Lotus Root Stewed with Hijiki Seaweed			☑ pack into bento box

Make in advance: Lotus Root Stewed with Hijiki Seaweed.

Prep the night before: Set timer on rice cooker, if using. Make egg crepes.

Sushi Roll Bento

This is a hearty bento for one hungry person, or for a couple to share. Sushi rolls are not that hard to make, once you get the hang of them. They are great finger food. Here they are accompanied by a crunchy and fun sausage salad, and fresh fruit.

CONTENTS

- Sushi Rolls with Salmon and Cucumber
- Sausage Salad
- Fruit

Sushi Rolls with Salmon and Cucumber

2 SERVINGS (2 SUSHI ROLLS)

Sushi rice contains vinegar and salt, which help to keep the filling fresh. You should avoid using raw fish for any sushi that is meant to be eaten some time after it has been made. For these easy sushi rolls, I've used canned salmon with mayonnaise and cucumber. Canned tuna also works well.

The secrets to making sushi rolls are decisiveness and practice. Don't hesitate too much, and the more you make, the better your rolls will look.

3 oz (90g) canned salmon, well drained
1 Tbsp mayonnaise
2 sheets nori seaweed, 7 x 8 inches
  (18 x 20cm)
3 cups (600g) prepared sushi rice (see page 67)
a few strips cut cucumber

Mix the salmon with the mayonnaise to form a paste.

Make ready a sushi rolling mat or a moistened and wrung-out clean kitchen towel, a cup of water with a little vinegar, and a very sharp knife.

Lay a sheet of nori seaweed shiny side down on the sushi mat or moistened kitchen towel (1).

Spread half the rice over the nori, leaving a 1 inch (2.5cm) gap at the end furthest away from you. Use moistened fingers to press out the rice evenly (2).

Place half the salmon paste on the rice as shown in the photograph, leaving a gap of about 1 inch (2.5cm) from the near edge (3).

Place a few cucumber strips on top of the salmon (4).

Roll the sushi mat or kitchen towel over the rice and squeeze firmly (5).

Pull the far end of the sushi mat or towel free of the rice with one hand, and continue rolling with the other. Squeeze evenly and firmly over the sushi mat or towel (6).

1   2

3   4

5

6

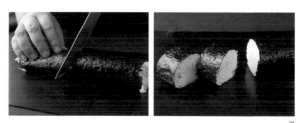

7

Mentally divide the sushi roll into 5 or 6 even pieces (you can use a ruler for this if you want to be precise). Make tiny cuts with the point of your knife to show where to slice the roll. Dip the knife in the cup of vinegar water and shake the excess drops off. Cut the sushi roll in one smooth stroke. Moisten the knife and repeat (7). Repeat the process for the second roll.

BENTO-FRIENDLY SUSHI-ROLL VARIATIONS
A sushi roll only needs one or two tasty fillings to be good. Try any of these easy fillings for rolls that will keep well until lunchtime and beyond.

- Classic California roll: strips of avocado, imitation crabmeat, and cucumber
- Smoked salmon, sliced onion, and cream cheese, often called a New York roll (adding butterhead lettuce makes this a Boston roll)
- Canned tuna mixed with mayonnaise and Tabasco sauce
- Strips of boiled or baked ham, cheese, and shredded lettuce
- Grilled salmon skin and radish sprouts
- Any soboro (see Soboro Bento, page 43)

Sausage Salad

4 SERVINGS

This salad is based on a classic Swiss-German lunch standby called Wurstsalat. Instead of using the usual mayonnaise, I've made it with a honey-mustard dressing. Some of the sausages are cut into fish shapes, an inspiration I had when I made this bento for a beach outing.

For the salad
1 medium English cucumber, de-seeded
1 celery stalk with leaves
10–12 cherry tomatoes
8 cocktail franks, or 3 hotdog franks

For the dressing
1 Tbsp apple cider vinegar
1 tsp sea salt
2 Tbsp olive oil
1 Tbsp honey
1 Tbsp Dijon-style mustard
black pepper, to taste

Cut the cucumber and celery into chunks. Leave the cherry tomatoes whole or cut into halves or quarters, depending on their size.

Put the dressing ingredients in a jar and shake well to combine. Mix with the vegetables. This part of the salad can be made up to 3 days in advance and stored in the refrigerator.

Cut a few of the sausages into fish shapes, following the diagram below. Chop the rest into bite-sized pieces. Boil the sausages for a couple of minutes, until the fish "tail" curls up. Drain and let cool.

Mix the cooled sausages with the vegetables. Decorate the salad with the fish-shaped sausages.

VARIATION: *This salad also tastes delicious if you mix in 1 oz (30g) Swiss cheese, diced small. You might be surprised at how well the creamy yet slightly acid flavors of cheese of complement the flavors in a sushi roll.*

SAUSAGE-FISH CUTTING DIAGRAM
score the top in a crisscross pattern

remove this part

make a hole and poke in a black sesame seed for eye (optional)

cut along dotted line

TIMELINE

The salad can be made in advance. The sushi roll tastes best if made in the morning.

MINUTES	10	5	0
Sushi Rolls with Salmon and Cucumber	☑ mix sushi vinegar into warm rice	☑ make sushi roll, cut up	
		☑ mix salmon and mayo, cut cucumber	☑ pack into bento box
Sausage Salad			☑ pack into bento box
Fruit			☑ pack into bento box

Prep the night before: Set timer on rice cooker, if using. Sausage Salad.

NOT-SO-JAPANESE BENTOS

A bento doesn't need to be filled with Japanese food to be called a bento. My rule: as long as it tastes and looks great at lunchtime, it's a bento. Here are some of my favorite not-so-Japanese bento combinations, with recipes inspired by cuisines from around the world.

Bunny Sandwich Bento

Who says that sandwiches have to be boring? If you take a few minutes to cut your everyday sandwich into cute shapes, as in this spring-themed bunny sandwich bento, lunch seems a whole lot more interesting.

CONTENTS

- Bunny Sandwiches
- Sausage and Cucumber Tulips
- Apple Bunnies
- Salad Greens and Cherry Tomatoes
- Dressing of Your Choice

Bunny Sandwiches

1 SERVING

2 tsp softened butter
2 small slices whole wheat bread
2 slices of ham
1 slice sandwich cheese
1 Tbsp cream cheese
2 Tbsp strawberry jam
2 small slices white bread
salad greens to line the box
cherry tomatoes, for garnish
parsley, for garnish

Spread the softened butter on one side of each slice of the whole wheat bread. Place the ham and cheese on the whole wheat bread and put together to form a sandwich. Spread cream cheese and jam on the white bread and put together to form a sandwich. Press down lightly on each sandwich so that the fillings adhere and the sandwich won't fall apart.

Make cutouts with a cookie cutter of your choice. Here I've cut out bunny shapes from each sandwich. To ensure that the sandwiches won't fall apart, skewer them with a strategically placed decorative cocktail stick (making sure that it doesn't look like the bunny has a stake in it!).

Line the bento box with the salad greens and arrange the sandwiches, tomatoes, and parsley on top.

TIP: *Don't let the leftover bits of sandwich go to waste after you've cut them into cute shapes. Toast them lightly in a nonstick frying pan and serve them for breakfast.*

Sausage and Cucumber Tulips

1 SERVING

These are fun to eat as well as being decorative.

2–3 cocktail franks or hotdog franks
1 medium English cucumber
4–5 cocktail sticks

If using cocktail franks, make zigzag incisions with a small, sharp knife around the middle of each frank. When you have gone all the way around, pull the halves apart carefully. If using hotdog franks, use just ½ inch (1cm) of each end of the sausage and make similar cuts. Reserve the rest of the sausage for another dish.

Put the cut sausage pieces in a pan and cover with water. Bring to a boil for a minute, until the "petals" of the tulip open up a little. Drain and let cool.

To make the leaves, cut a cucumber in half lengthwise and remove any seeds or pith inside with the tip of a spoon. Slice the halves into 1 inch (2.5cm) long pieces.

Take one piece and cut out a deep V from one end. Cut the corners off the other end, again in a V shape. You should end up with a fat, V-shaped piece.

To assemble the tulip, pierce up through the center of the V-shaped cucumber and the sausage "flower" with a cocktail stick.

AHEAD-OF-TIME NOTE: *The tulips can be made the night before, and the salad greens washed and dried beforehand.*

Apple Bunnies

MAKES 8

Every Japanese girl grows up somehow knowing how to cut these cute bunny-shaped apple wedges. They may seem rather fiddly, but with practice you'll be able to whip out one to decorate your bento in no time.

2 cups (480ml) cold water
½ tsp salt or juice of half a lemon
1 apple, preferably red-skinned

Place the cold water in a bowl. Add the salt or lemon juice.

With a small sharp knife, cut an apple (a red-skinned one gives the most striking effect) in half, and each half into 4 wedges.

Cut out the core of 1 wedge. With your knife, mark a point in the middle of the wedge on the skin side. Above this point, mark 2 points, one on each side of the apple wedge, about 1 inch (2.5cm) from the end of the wedge and parallel to each other. Make a shallow V-cut connecting each of these side points to the center point.

Carefully peel away the skin that is in the middle of the V-shaped incision. I find this works best if I carefully pry up the mid-point of the V first with the tip of the knife.

Once this V-shaped section of skin is removed, slide the knife blade under each of the remaining points down to the mid-point mark, taking care not to cut the skin off. These will be the "ears" of the bunny.

Put the cut bunny wedge into the salted or lemon water and leave until the ears curl up a bit. The water will also prevent the apple from turning brown.

Repeat for as many apple bunnies as you want to make.

TO ASSEMBLE THIS BENTO

Arrange lettuce leaves and other greens in a bento box. Make sure the leaves don't have any droplets of water on them. Arrange the sandwiches, tulips, and apple bunnies on the greens. Fill the gaps with parsley and cherry tomatoes. Pack a container of dressing separately.

Pre-assembled Sandwiches

Sandwiches that are assembled in the morning should either have a high-fat moisture barrier between the filling and the bread, or the filling itself should be high fat (such as nut butter), or low moisture (such as jam).

The best moisture-barrier spread for sandwiches is softened butter. The butter can be flavored beforehand by mixing in ingredients such as mustard for an extra kick. You can also use margarine, cream cheese, peanut butter, and other nut butters. The classic American combination of peanut butter and jelly is a perfect sandwich filler, since it's both high in fat and low in moisture.

Other cut-out sandwich filling suggestions include tuna salad prepared with mayonnaise between buttered bread; jam and butter; thinly sliced corned beef or other canned meats; and cream cheese with smoked salmon or chives.

Cut-out sandwiches are best made with soft sliced bread and finely textured, easy-to-cut fillings such as spreads, cheese, thinly sliced vegetables, and boiled ham.

TIMELINE

MINUTES	15	10	5	0
Bunny Sandwiches	☑ soften butter and cream cheese for 10 seconds in microwave		☑ assemble sandwiches and cut out	☑ pack into bento box with tomatoes and parsley
Sausage and Cucumber Tulips	☑ cut sausages ☑ let cool ☑ boil sausages		☑ cut cucumber and assemble tulips	☑ pack into bento box
Apple Bunnies	☑ make ready bowl of lemon or salted water	☑ cut apple wedge and make bunny	☑ put apple bunny in lemon or salted water	☑ pack into bento box

Prep the night before: Wash and dry salad greens.
Line bento box with greens, cover, and place in refrigerator.
Set out knife, cocktail sticks, cutting board.

Sandwich Bentos

Assemble-at-lunch Sandwich Bentos

For hearty sandwiches with lots of fillings, I prefer to pack the fixings separately from the bread. This approach has several advantages. It prevents the bread from getting soggy by lunchtime, allows you to use any crumbly, hard-to-slice, or chunky filling that you want, and sidesteps the need to butter your bread beforehand unless you want to. It's like getting a freshly made sandwich at the deli, but with your own fillings and sides. Just take care to pack any foods that may need to be kept cool, including butter or mayonnaise, with an ice pack. (Tip: pack a single portion of butter in a small, lidded condiment container.) Note that this type of sandwich may not be suitable for very young children. For older kids, you could try including written assembly instructions for fun.

SOME EXAMPLES

- Homemade meatloaf slices packed with ketchup on the side; a container of salad greens, tomato, and onion slices; a small box of fresh fruit; and 2 slices of whole wheat bread (homemade, if possible!).
- Slices of leftover roast beef with juices in a leakproof bento box, leftover roasted vegetables, a small container of mustard, fresh watercress leaves in a separate container or ziplock bag, a crusty sesame roll split in half, and a brownie for dessert.
- Slices of chicken breast from a roast chicken dinner the night before, a small packet of mayonnaise, coleslaw in a container packed with an ice pack, and a third of a baguette sliced down the middle and wrapped in plastic with the cut sides together to keep the exposed bread from drying out.

Assemble-at-lunch Banh Mi Sandwich Bento
1 SERVING

A great assemble-at-lunch sandwich is the Vietnamese banh mi sandwich—a crispy baguette roll that is hollowed out and toasted, then filled with shredded vegetables, meat or other protein, and mayonnaise.

For the bread
1 small baguette roll, or a 7 inch (18cm) cut length of a long baguette
2 tsp butter
1 tsp Vietnamese fish sauce, or soy sauce

For the filling
1 cup (110g) shredded vegetables consisting of 1 or more of the following:
    cucumber
    daikon radish or red radish
    turnip
    carrot
    cabbage
3 jalapeño or other mildly hot peppers, de-seeded and thinly sliced
2 tsp Vietnamese fish sauce or soy sauce
1 Tbsp rice vinegar
pinch salt
2 oz (60g) shredded cooked meat, or pâté
1 Tbsp mayonnaise

Preheat the oven to 400°F (200°C), or use a toaster oven if you have one, on the "bagel" setting. Cut the baguette in half lengthwise and scoop out the soft insides (reserve these to use as breadcrumbs in another dish). Spread the inside of the scooped-out bread shells with the butter, and drizzle on the fish sauce or soy sauce. (It may be blasphemy, but I think that half a teaspoon of Marmite—the savory yeast spread from England that people either love or hate—works best here.) Toast until the scooped-out baguette is lightly crisped on the inside. Let cool completely, then wrap in foil.

For the filling, combine the vegetables with the soy sauce or fish sauce, rice vinegar, and salt.

Pack the meat or pâté in a bento divider cup, and put the cup in the bento box. Put mayonnaise in a sauce cup. Fill the rest of the bento box with the seasoned vegetables. Pack the bread separately.

At lunchtime, spread the mayonnaise on the bread. Combine the meat and vegetables and mound onto the bread. If using pâté, spread that on the bread, then add the vegetables. Eat leaning over your bento box to catch the drips!

Edge-sealed Pocket Sandwich

In Japan, sliced-bread sandwiches are almost always crustless, and Pocket Sandwiches are a variation on these.

Use slices of soft white or whole wheat bread to make sandwiches with the filling of your choice, taking care to not let the filling extend all the way to the edges of the bread. Using a rigid plastic container that is a bit smaller than the sandwich, press down on the assembled sandwich firmly. This cuts and seals the edges of the bread at the same time. You can buy sandwich-cutting equipment that is expressly made for this purpose from bento accessory suppliers.

Deconstructed Salade Niçoise Bento

Salade Niçoise is a classic composed salad that originates from the sunny town of Nice in the south of France. It's perfect for a summer bento lunch.

Deconstructed Salade Niçoise

1 SERVING

1 medium potato
2 Tbsp extra virgin olive oil
6–8 quail eggs, or 1 chicken egg
2 tsp red wine vinegar
1 tsp Dijon-style mustard
salt and pepper, to taste
5–6 cherry tomatoes
3 oz (90g) canned tuna (preferably packed in olive oil for optimum flavor)
1 Tbsp capers, optional
3–4 black olives, preferably Niçoise or Kalamata
salad greens and lettuce

Make ready three bento boxes: a large one to hold the lettuce and greens; a medium one for the potato, eggs, and tomatoes; and a small one for the tuna, olives, and dressing that fits inside the large one if possible.

Wash, peel, and cut up the potato into ½ inch (1cm) cubes. Put the potato pieces in a small pan and add enough cold salted water to cover. Boil until tender, about 10 minutes. Drain well. Coat lightly with 1 teaspoon of the olive oil.

Carefully pierce the rounded end of each quail egg with a thin needle before boiling; this will make them easier to peel. Quail eggs only need to be boiled for 4 minutes to achieve the hard-boiled state. (If using a chicken egg, see boiling instructions on page 60.) Peel the eggs.

Make a simple vinaigrette by combining the rest of the olive oil, the vinegar, mustard, salt, and pepper in the small bento box. Mix well.

TO ASSEMBLE THIS BENTO

Put the potato and eggs in the medium bento box. Decorate with the cherry tomatoes. Put the well-drained tuna, the capers, and the olives in the small bento box with the vinaigrette.

Fill the largest bento box with the salad greens and lettuce. Nestle the small bento box in the greens, and put on the lid. You may want to pack everything together with an ice pack in hot weather.

When ready to eat, simply put all the salad components into the large bento box: the potato and eggs first, and the tuna mixture on top. Mix well and enjoy!

TIMELINE

Prepare the potato, eggs, and tuna the night before and store in the refrigerator. Wash and dry the salad greens beforehand also. Pack the greens into the bento box in the morning for optimum freshness.

If you eat a lot of salads, you could make vinaigrette in quantity and stock it in the refrigerator. I like to use a screw-top jar for this, and give it a good shake before using.

VARIATION RECIPES

Salad Bentos

There's nothing better than a hearty salad bento on a hot summer's day.

Caponata Pasta Salad

1 SERVING

Caponata is a famous sauce or condiment from Sicily. Its sweet, sour, and savory flavors are delicious hot or cold, making it perfect as a base for a pasta salad bento.

salad greens and lettuce
½ teaspoon olive oil
½ cup (200g) Caponata (see page 80)
1 cup (140g) cooked short pasta such as macaroni, farfalle, or penne
cherry tomatoes, for garnish
olives, for garnish

Line a large bento box with the salad greens, as for the Salade Niçoise bento.

Drizzle the olive oil or a little of the oily part of the Caponata onto the pasta while the pasta is still hot, and toss well to coat. Let cool completely, then pack into a small container that fits inside the large bento box. The pasta should not touch the salad leaves until you are ready to eat, otherwise the leaves may turn limp. Pack the pasta salad into a bento divider cup, garnished with the cherry tomatoes and olives. When you are ready to eat, mix the caponata with the pasta and arrange on top of the salad greens.

Caponata

6–12 SERVINGS

Caponata is wonderful as a pasta sauce, a dip, or a sandwich spread or filling. It keeps for a week in the refrigerator, or for up to 3 months in the freezer.

1 large or 2 medium eggplants, cut into ½ inch (1cm) cubes
salt, for sprinkling
½ cup (120ml) olive oil
1 large onion, roughly chopped
1 small carrot, roughly chopped
1 celery stalk, roughly chopped
4 garlic cloves, sliced
4 cans (each 15 oz [425g]) whole peeled tomatoes, crushed
1 Tbsp dried or 2 Tbsp fresh thyme
1 bay leaf
1 Tbsp red chili flakes, or to taste
4 Tbsp golden raisins
2 Tbsp balsamic vinegar
3 Tbsp capers
2 Tbsp pine nuts, toasted in a dry frying pan for a few minutes
salt and pepper, to taste

Sprinkle the eggplant cubes with salt and leave to drain in a colander for 20 minutes.

In the meantime, heat 2 tablespoons of the olive oil in a heavy-bottomed pan over medium-high heat. Sauté the onion, carrot, and celery until the onion is translucent. Add the garlic and sauté until softened. Add the canned tomatoes and raise the heat to high to bring to a boil. Turn the heat to medium-low, add the thyme, bay leaf, and chili, and simmer for 30 minutes.

While the tomato sauce is simmering, squeeze out excess moisture from the salted eggplant. Heat up a large frying pan over medium-high heat and add the remaining olive oil. Sauté the eggplant cubes until softened and slightly browned, using more olive oil if needed.

Add the sautéed eggplant, raisins, and balsamic vinegar to the tomato sauce and simmer for an additional 15–20 minutes. Add the capers and toasted pine nuts. Taste, and season with pepper and more salt if needed.

Cucumber, Dill, and Smoked Trout Salad Bento

1 SERVING

This is a very refreshing warm-weather bento. The components are carried separately, then mixed together just before eating for the best texture and flavor. Carry the cucumber salad in a container with an ice pack if you can, to keep it cool and crunchy until lunchtime. You can substitute your favorite smoked fish for the trout.

½ English cucumber, de-seeded and sliced
pinch salt
1 medium potato, boiled in salted water and cut into ½ inch (1cm) dice
2 rye crisp crackers
butter pat, for crackers
2½ oz (70g) smoked trout, mackerel, or other smoked fish, deboned, skinned, and cut into chunks

For the dressing
2 Tbsp roughly chopped fresh dill
1 Tbsp finely chopped celery
1 Tbsp white wine vinegar
2 tsp honey
⅛ tsp salt
1 Tbsp Greek yogurt

Place the cucumber in a colander and sprinkle with the salt. Allow to stand for 10 minutes. Squeeze the cucumber lightly.

Combine the dressing ingredients in a bowl. Add the cucumber, and leave to marinate overnight.

When packing the bento, use three separate containers: one for the cucumber salad, one for the potato, and one for the flaked, smoked fish. Pack the crackers in a plastic bag or paper napkin. When you are ready to eat, mix the smoked fish and potatoes with the cucumber salad.

VARIATION: *Use lemon juice instead of vinegar in the salad dressing.*

Taco Rice Bento

1 SERVING

Taco rice is a Japanese-American fusion dish that was first invented in Okinawa, Japan's southernmost island chain. The dish takes typical Tex-Mex taco fillings and combines them with plain rice instead of corn tortillas. It makes an interesting and satisfying salad-style bento. It is often served with a fried egg on top.

1 cup (200g) cooked Basic White Rice (see page 53)
½ cup Taco Meat Filling (see facing page)
3 Tbsp shredded cheddar cheese
1 cup (75g) shredded romaine or iceberg lettuce
⅓ English cucumber, de-seeded and cut into ¼ inch (0.5cm) dice
½ cup (225g) Fresh Tomato Salsa (see facing page)

Make ready two bento boxes: one to hold the rice and taco meat filling, and the other to hold the salad ingredients.

Pack the rice into one bento box. Place the taco meat filling on top. Scatter with shredded cheese. Pack the shredded lettuce and diced cucumber in the other bento box, along with the salsa, packed in a small inner cup. (You should carry this box with an ice pack if possible.)

To eat, layer the vegetables on top of the rice and taco meat filling, and pour the salsa on top.

VARIATION: *If you still want the crunch of corn tortillas, carry a small bag of chips with your bento, crush the chips, and scatter them on top of the vegetables.*

Taco Meat Filling
6–12 SERVINGS

This filling can be used for regular flour or corn tortillas as well as on top of rice. It's a great bento staple to stash in your freezer.

1 Tbsp vegetable oil	2 Tbsp tomato paste
2 large onions, finely chopped	1 Tbsp ground cumin
2 celery stalks, finely chopped	1 Tbsp red chili flakes, or to taste
3 garlic cloves, finely chopped	1 Tbsp ground coriander
2 lb (900g) finely ground lean beef	½ Tbsp dried oregano
2 cans (each 15 oz [425g]) crushed tomatoes	½ Tbsp dried thyme
3 pickled jalapeño chilies, drained, stems removed, and roughly chopped	salt and black pepper, to taste

Heat the oil in large frying pan over medium-high heat. Add the onions, celery, and garlic, and sauté until the onions are translucent. Remove the sautéed vegetables from the frying pan, turn the heat to high, and add the ground beef. Sauté until the meat is browned, and drain away any excess fat in the pan.

Return the sautéed vegetables to the pan, together with the canned tomatoes, jalapeño chilies, tomato paste, herbs, and spices. Cook over medium heat until the mixture has thickened. Season with salt and black pepper.

This can be stored in the refrigerator for a week, and in the freezer for up to 3 months. I like to divide the mixture into single-use portions (about ½ cup [120g]) and freeze in small plastic freezer containers or ziplock bags.

Fresh Tomato Salsa
MAKES 2–3 CUPS (450–675G)

Fresh tomato salsa tastes so much better than store-bought. This keeps in the refrigerator for 3–4 days.

2 large ripe yet firm tomatoes
1 small red onion
2 jalapeño peppers
½ cup (10g) chopped fresh coriander leaves
1 Tbsp lime juice
salt and pepper, to taste
a few dashes of red pepper sauce, optional

Cut the tomatoes in half. Cut out the core, and remove the seeds and the watery parts around the seeds. Cut the tomatoes into small dice. Chop the red onion very finely. De-seed and de-vein the jalapeños and chop finely.

Combine all the ingredients and mix well. Leave for at least an hour before eating to allow the flavors to blend. Add a few dashes of red pepper sauce if you want it spicier.

Salad Bento Rules

- Make sure greens are dried thoroughly after washing. Wet greens can not only turn soggy, they spoil a lot faster too.
- Pack cut, raw vegetables and salad greens separately from other ingredients such as egg, tuna, cheese, and cold cuts. Keep greens cool with an ice pack.
- Use cherry tomatoes rather than slices of large tomatoes. Cherry tomatoes are usually sweeter, especially out of season, and a lot less watery. If using large tomatoes, de-seed them.
- Always pack dressing and leafy greens separately. Pouring dressing over raw leafy vegetables such as lettuce too far in advance will turn them soggy.
- Bread and crackers should also be packed separately.
- For small children, make sure that the vegetables are cut into bite-sized pieces, or pieces that can be eaten easily with the hands.
- Consider keeping a bottle of dressing in the office refrigerator, or some packets of dressing that do not need refrigeration in your desk drawer.
- If you are using mayonnaise, make sure to keep it cool with an ice pack to avoid spoilage. Mayonnaise can be packed in a sealable sauce cup; ready-sealed individual packets of mayonnaise are also handy for bentos.
- I don't like the way that the pasta in a typical pasta salad turns limp and soggy over time. To retain its texture, coat the pasta with a little oil and make sure it is completely cool before packing. Always pack the sauce or dressing separately, and mix just before eating.

Pan-fried Chicken Nugget Bento

Kids and adults alike love chicken nuggets. My lighter-than-usual version is coated with a crispy cornflake crust instead of a thick batter, and pan-fried rather than deep-fried. The nuggets are accompanied by potato salad rather than French fries, plus lots of crunchy vegetables with an almost no-calorie dipping sauce.

CONTENTS

- Pan-fried Chicken Nuggets
- Potato Salad
- Vegetable Crudités with Citrus-herb Sauce

Pan-fried Chicken Nuggets

1 SERVING

These are quite low in fat, making them perfect for people watching their waistlines. The cornflake crust adds some sweetness, and mayonnaise is used as a simple undercoating to help the cornflakes adhere to the chicken. The mayonnaise also adds a tangy flavor. Take care not to overcook the nuggets, since white chicken meat can get dry.

4 oz (120g) boneless, skinless chicken breast
salt and pepper, to taste
1 Tbsp reduced-fat mayonnaise
½ cup (30g) crushed cornflakes
2 tsp vegetable oil

Cut the chicken into bite-sized pieces. Season with the salt and pepper.

In a small bowl, coat the chicken thoroughly with the mayonnaise. Put the crushed cornflakes in a plastic bag, and then put in the mayonnaise-coated chicken. Shake the bag to coat the chicken with the cornflakes.

Heat the oil in a small nonstick frying pan over medium heat. When the pan is hot, add the chicken. Fry on both sides until the chicken feels firm when pressed. Put the chicken pieces on paper towels to drain away excess oil. Let cool completely before packing.

Potato Salad

1 SERVING

This is my favorite kind of potato salad—a Japanese version with mayonnaise and without the assertive vinegar flavor of German-style potato salads for example—although I've cut the calories a bit by using reduced-fat mayonnaise. For a really authentic Japanese potato salad, try to get hold of a Japanese brand of mayonnaise. Japanese mayonnaise is very rich and thick, with more egg yolk content than most American or European brands.

small piece cucumber
salt, for sprinkling
1 medium potato
1 inch (2.5cm) length carrot
2 Tbsp reduced-fat mayonnaise
salt and pepper, to taste

De-seed and thinly slice the cucumber. Sprinkle with a little salt, and massage with your hands until the cucumber is limp. Squeeze out the excess moisture.

Wash the potato. With a knife, score a line around the middle of the potato. Wrap the potato in a paper towel, then in plastic wrap. Wrap the carrot in plastic wrap.

Microwave the potato and carrot on high for 3 minutes. Unwrap the potato and, using the paper towel to protect your hands, pull the skin off gently.

If you don't have a microwave, boil the potato and carrot until tender in salted water.

Cut the potato into ½ inch (1cm) cubes. Cut the carrot in half and slice into thin half-rounds. Place in a small bowl and mix with the mayonnaise and a little salt and pepper. Fold in the sliced cucumber. Let cool, and pack into a cupcake liner or bento divider cup.

AHEAD-OF-TIME NOTE: *This salad can be made the night before.*

Vegetable Crudités with Citrus-herb Sauce

MAKES ½ CUP (120ML)

The light, tangy sauce is a Westernized take on a citrusy Japanese sauce called *ponzu*. It also makes a great non-oil dressing for salads.

For the sauce

¼ cup (60ml) chicken or vegetable stock

3 Tbsp lemon juice

1 Tbsp balsamic vinegar

pinch each dried thyme and oregano

¼ tsp sea salt, or to taste

black pepper, to taste

For the vegetable sticks

Raw vegetables of your choice, cut into sticks or bite-sized pieces. (Here I have used cucumber, celery, carrots, and strips of red pepper.)

Put all the sauce ingredients into a jar or shaker, and shake well until combined. Store any leftover sauce in the refrigerator in a nonreactive (glass or ceramic, never metal) container with a tight-fitting lid, where it will keep for up to a week. (I prefer to use homemade, sodium-free stock for its superior taste, but use whatever you have on hand. If using store-bought salted stock, adjust the amount of salt you add accordingly.)

TO ASSEMBLE THIS BENTO

Put the sauce in a separate small container with a tight-fitting, leakproof lid. Arrange the carrot and celery sticks neatly. Put the potato salad in a cup, and the chicken in the remaining space.

VARIATION RECIPE

Ground Chicken Nuggets

MAKES **10–12**

These light, almost bouncy, chicken nuggets are made with finely ground chicken meat rather than whole pieces of chicken as in the Pan-fried Chicken Nuggets, and take more time to prepare. It's worth making batches in advance, however, as they freeze very well. They can be deep-fried, pan-fried, or oven-baked straight from the freezer. A food processor is recommended.

¼ medium onion, roughly chopped

4 inch (10cm) length celery stalk, roughly chopped

2 inch (5cm) length carrot, roughly chopped

1 lb (450g) boneless, skinless chicken breast, cut into 1 inch (2.5cm) chunks

1 egg

½ tsp salt, or to taste

black pepper, to taste

1–2 Tbsp cornstarch

flour, for coating

oil, for frying

If using a food processor, use the chopping blade to process the onion, celery, and carrot until very finely chopped. Remove from the food processor and set aside. Put the cut-up chicken breast in the food processor. Process until finely ground. Add the vegetables, and pulse until combined. Add the egg, salt and pepper, and 1 tablespoon of cornstarch, and pulse to form a smooth, fluffy paste. If the paste is too runny to hold its shape in a spoon, add more cornstarch.

If you don't have a food processor, grate the vegetables finely, and use finely ground chicken or turkey. Mix the ingredients together well with your hands.

To form the nuggets, put the flour onto a plate. Drop spoonfuls of the chicken mixture onto the flour and turn carefully to coat them on all sides. At this point you can put the nuggets into the refrigerator to firm them up a bit—this makes them easier to cook, especially if you are going to bake or pan-fry them.

To deep-fry the nuggets, heat your frying oil to 340°F (170°C). Fry 2 or 3 at a time until a light golden brown, and drain well.

To pan-fry the nuggets, heat a little cooking oil in a large frying pan. Flatten out the nuggets slightly. Cook on both sides for 3–4 minutes until browned.

To bake the nuggets, preheat the oven to 350°F (175°C). Coat the bottom of a baking dish with a little cooking oil. Place the nuggets in the baking dish and drizzle a little oil over the top. Bake for 10 minutes, turn, and bake for an additional 5 minutes.

The nuggets can be made the day before and stored in the refrigerator. Reheat them in the morning in a dry frying pan over medium heat for 2–3 minutes on each side, or in a toaster oven for 5–6 minutes. They can be frozen for up to a month. Frozen nuggets can be cooked straight from the freezer. Allow 4–5 minutes for deep-frying, 8–10 minutes for baking or pan-frying.

MORE CHICKEN NUGGET VARIATIONS

- Spicy Chicken Nuggets: Add ½ teaspoon of chili powder to the chicken mix.
- Curry-flavored Chicken Nuggets: Put 1 teaspoon of curry powder in a dry frying pan over medium heat, and stir for 2–3 minutes to dry-roast it and bring out the flavors. Add the curry powder to the nugget mixture.
- Honey-mustard Chicken Nuggets: Combine 1 tablespoon of Dijon-style mustard and 1 teaspoon of honey in a dry frying pan over low heat. Put the freshly cooked nuggets into the pan and coat with the sauce. Alternatively, pack the honey-mustard sauce separately to use as a dipping sauce.
- Poppy-seed Chicken Nuggets: Dip the floured nuggets in beaten egg, then roll in white or black poppy seeds. You can use sesame seeds instead of poppy seeds.

Using Bentos for Weight Loss

Incorporating healthy homemade bentos into your weight-loss program is a great idea. Their compact size makes portion control easier, and also means you don't get into the bad habit of eating fast food and high-calorie snack food for lunch—one of the main reasons I started making bentos for myself.

Bento boxes may seem too small to satisfy an adult appetite, but if you pack them tightly they do hold more food than you may think. Experiment by putting a typical meal that's part of your weight-loss program into a bento box—or, if you don't have a bento box yet, a small plastic container. Except for items that need lots of air around them, like fresh salads, most food can be packed into a small container quite efficiently. See pages 114–116 for more about different types of bento boxes and recommended sizes.

Although bentos help with portion control, the type of food you pack still matters. You can pack plenty of calories into even the tiniest box if you aren't paying attention! You can, however, include tiny portions of high-calorie foods in a bento box as a treat, as long as you balance them out with lower-calorie foods. For instance, I occasionally like to tuck a chocolate truffle in one corner of my bento as an extra-special dessert. Even the richest chocolate truffle is less than 100 calories.

Don't underestimate the amount of food you really need to keep your energy levels up. Some people, especially young girls, choose tiny bento boxes meant to be used by kindergarten children or as side boxes. These little boxes are cute, but they do not hold much food, and hunger pains may lead you straight to the vending machine a few hours later. On the other hand, using these tiny boxes for snack bentos to eat between meals is a great idea.

Always consult with a medical professional before starting any weight-loss program.

TIMELINE

The Vegetable Crudités and Potato Salad can be prepared the night before, and the Citrus-herb Sauce can be made up to a week in advance. Make the chicken in the morning for optimum flavor. Be sure to let the chicken pieces cool completely before packing.

MINUTES	15	10	5	0
Pan-fried Chicken Nuggets	☑ cut up chicken ☑ heat up frying pan with oil	☑ coat chicken in mayonnaise and cornflakes ☑ cook chicken	☑ let cool	☑ pack into bento box
Potato Salad			☑ mix vegetables, mayonnaise, and seasonings ☑ pack into bento divider cup	
Vegetable Crudités and bento assembly				☑ arrange crudités, inner containers, and chicken nuggets

Prep the night before: Citrus-herb Sauce.
Peel, cut, and boil potatoes.
Cut up vegetables for Potato Salad.
Cut up vegetable crudités, put in bento box and cover, store in refrigerator.
Crush cornflakes in plastic bag.

Mediterranean Mezze-style Bento

A mezze is a selection of appetizers, seen in various cuisines around the Mediterranean. This bento is a mini version of a mezze, with two kinds of dip, a simple fresh salad, and koftas—soft meatballs made of lamb or beef.

CONTENTS

- Lamb or Beef Koftas
- Baba Ghanoush
- Edamame Hummus
- Parsley, Tomato, and Cucumber Salad
- Pita Bread

Lamb or Beef Koftas

4–5 SERVINGS (24 SMALL KOFTA)

Koftas are soft, flavorful Middle Eastern–style meatballs. They are sold as street food, and are usually grilled, but you can also bake or pan-fry them. I do suggest using a food processor to achieve the desired smooth texture with ease.

1 small onion
1 lb (450g) ground beef or lamb
¼ cup (5g) roughly chopped flat leaf parsley, leaves only
2 Tbsp roughly chopped fresh coriander leaves
1 tsp ground cumin
1 tsp salt
black pepper, to taste
olive oil, for drizzling
greens to line the bento

To mix in a food processor, cut the onion into wedges. Insert the chopping blade in your food processor and chop up the onion finely. Remove the onion and set aside. Put the meat in the food processor. Pulse until it is ground to a finer texture. Add the rest of the ingredients and pulse to mix well.

To hand mix, get the butcher to double-grind the meat for you in order to achieve a smooth texture. Chop the parsley and coriander leaves as finely as possible. Chop the onion very finely, or grate it with a handheld grater. Mix all the ingredients together with your hands until combined.

To form the koftas, divide the meat mixture into about 24 small, flattened balls. Heat up a stovetop grill pan or frying pan over medium-high heat, or preheat the oven to 350°F (175°C). Drizzle a little olive oil over the balls, and turn to coat in the oil.

Grill or pan-fry the koftas for about 5 minutes until browned on the bottom side. Turn and cook for an additional 4–5 minutes on the other side until they are browned all over and cooked through. Alternatively, bake in the oven at 350°F (175°C) for 25–30 minutes.

Pack the koftas on a bed of greens.

AHEAD-OF-TIME NOTE: *Koftas freeze very nicely, cooked or raw. They can also be made the day before and kept in the refrigerator.*

Baba Ghanoush

6 SERVINGS

This is a delicious dip made with baked eggplant. It will keep in the refrigerator for several days, so make it a day or two before you need it.

1 large or 5 small eggplants
　(to yield 2 cups [340g] eggplant pulp before draining)
3 Tbsp tahini or sesame paste
2 cloves Roasted Garlic (see page 88)
⅓ cup (80g) lemon juice
1 tsp salt
extra virgin olive oil, for drizzling
paprika or shichimi pepper, for decoration, optional

Preheat the oven to 400°F (200°C). Prick the eggplant all over with a fork. Place on a baking sheet and bake for 30–40 minutes, until the skin is brown and the eggplant itself is somewhat shriveled. Take out and let cool.

When cool, cut in half and scrape out the flesh into a colander. Let the excess moisture drain off for 15–20 minutes.

Put the eggplant and the rest of the ingredients into a food processor. Process until smooth.

Let rest in the refrigerator, well covered, for at least several hours to allow the flavors to mellow.

Pack into a small container that fits into your bento box and drizzle a little olive oil on top. To add some color, sprinkle on a little paprika or shichimi pepper.

AHEAD-OF-TIME NOTE: *This keeps in the refrigerator for a week. It can also be frozen.*

Edamame Hummus

4 SERVINGS

This is a twist on the traditional bean dip, hummus, which is usually made with chickpeas. I first saw edamame hummus at a deli in New York. I bought some because of the bright green color, but didn't actually like the taste—the sesame flavor of the tahini totally overwhelmed the edamame. This is my version, which I think retains the fresh flavor of the edamame better. A food processor is required for this recipe, to achieve a smooth consistency.

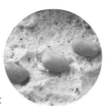

2 cups (150g) frozen or fresh shelled edamame beans
1 Tbsp tahini or sesame paste
1 Tbsp extra virgin olive oil
3 cloves Roasted Garlic (see below)
¼ cup (60ml) lime or lemon juice
1 tsp salt

Put the edamame in a pan and cover with water. Bring to a boil and cook until the beans are tender. Drain and cool under running water to fix the bright green color. Reserve 2 or 3 edamame to use as garnish.

Put all the ingredients into a food processor. Process until smooth. Taste, and adjust the seasoning if needed.

Pack into a small container that fits into your bento box. Garnish on top with the reserved whole edamame beans.

AHEAD-OF-TIME NOTE: *This keeps in the refrigerator for 3–4 days. It can also be frozen.*

Roasted Garlic

When garlic is roasted, it turns soft and mild and can be mashed into a spreadable paste with ease. It's great to use when the sharpness of raw garlic is undesirable. As a bonus, it doesn't give you garlic breath!

1 head garlic
olive oil, for sprinkling
salt, for sprinkling

Remove the outer skin from the head of garlic. Separate into cloves, and place the cloves, unpeeled, on a piece of aluminum foil. Sprinkle with olive oil and a little salt. Bake at 350°F (175°C) for 30 minutes, or until the garlic is soft. To use, squeeze the garlic out of the skins. Roasted garlic keeps in the refrigerator for a week, and can also be frozen for up to a month. To freeze, squeeze the softened garlic out of the skins and press flat in a plastic bag. Seal the bag well to store. Break off pieces to use when required.

Parsley, Tomato, and Cucumber Salad

1 SERVING

This is a very simple, fresh-tasting salad.

4-inch (10cm) length English cucumber
1 small tomato
⅓ cup (7g) roughly chopped flat leaf parsley, leaves only
1 tsp chopped fresh mint leaves
2 Tbsp lemon juice
2 tsp olive oil
salt and pepper, to taste

De-seed the cucumber if necessary by cutting it in half lengthwise and scooping out the seeds with the tip of a teaspoon. Slice the cucumber thinly. De-seed the tomato and cut into wedges.

Mix all the ingredients together. Allow to marinate overnight in the refrigerator for maximum flavor. This salad will keep in the refrigerator for 2–3 days.

Pack with an ice pack to keep the salad nice and cool.

TO PACK THIS BENTO

The flavors of each component of this bento should be kept separate until lunchtime, so pack them in small containers. Here I have used a bento box with little internal divider cups for the dips and I have packed the koftas in the main part of the box on a bed of salad greens. I've used a side box for the Parsley, Tomato, and Cucumber Salad. You could also use a series of small plastic boxes—part of the fun of putting a bento lunch together is figuring out which of your collection of various cute little containers to use. Bring your pita bread in a plastic ziplock bag or wrapped in a napkin that's large enough to envelop it completely, to prevent it from drying out.

TIMELINE

Note that while there is a lot of preparation to do, everything in this bento can be made in advance. The dips in fact taste better when made at least several hours before eating. Make them in quantity when you have some time, and freeze them in bento-sized portions.

Mezze-style Dishes

These Middle Eastern–inspired recipes will add color and spice to your bento.

Easy Classic Hummus
MAKES ABOUT 1¾ CUPS (440G)

Classic hummus is made from dried chickpeas that have been soaked then cooked. This easy version uses canned chickpeas and just a hint of garlic. Adjust the amount of lemon juice to your taste.

15 oz (425g) can chickpeas
1 garlic clove, grated finely or smashed to a paste
3 Tbsp tahini or sesame paste
3 Tbsp lemon juice
2 Tbsp olive oil
salt, to taste

Drain the chickpeas and rinse them in a colander under running water. Using a food processor, chop finely. Add the rest of the ingredients except for the salt, and process until a smooth paste is formed. Add salt to taste.
    This will keep in the refrigerator for up to a week.

Spicy Roasted Carrots
2 SERVING

Carrots that are slowly roasted become intensely rich and sweet. The added spices counteract the sweetness to make a delicious dish. Multiply the amounts and freeze the extras.

1 large or 2 medium carrots, cut into ½ inch (1cm) chunks
½ Tbsp olive oil
1 tsp honey
½ tsp ground cumin
½ tsp ground coriander leaves
¼ tsp black pepper
1 Tbsp chopped fresh coriander or flat leaf parsley
salt, to taste

Preheat the oven to 400°F (200°C). A toaster oven also works well for this recipe.
    In a small bowl, toss the carrot chunks with the other ingredients. Place the carrots in a baking dish and cook in the oven for 20–25 minutes, turning them a couple of times, or until they are very tender and caramelized on the outside. This will keep in the refrigerator for 2–3 days, and can also be frozen for up to a month.

To turn this into a roasted carrot spread to put on sandwiches or crackers, process in a food processor until smooth.

Fava Beans with Lemon-mint Dressing
2 SERVING

Fresh or frozen shelled edamame beans work well with this dressing too.

8 to 10 fava beans, shelled
pinch salt
1 tsp olive oil
1 tsp lemon juice
½ garlic clove, crushed
salt, to taste
1 fresh mint leaf, finely shredded

Put the fava beans in a small pan and cover with water. Add the pinch of salt. Bring to a boil over high heat, and boil for 3–4 minutes until tender. Drain and cool under running cold water. Peel off the skins.
    In a small bowl, combine the olive oil, lemon juice, crushed garlic, and salt. Add the fava beans and the mint leaf.
    This will keep in the refrigerator for 1–2 days. It does not freeze well.

Summer Vegetable Casserole Bento

This vegetarian bento is inspired by a picnic lunch I had a couple of summers ago in the heart of Provence, in the south of France. It has a portion of a traditional vegetable casserole known as a tian, which is delicious when cold, plus cheese, a zesty salad, and crusty bread. What could be better?

CONTENTS

- Provençal Vegetable Tian
- Beet Salad with Grainy Mustard Dressing
- Baby Salad Leaves or Mesclun Mix Greens
- Assorted Cheeses
- Whole-grain Bread Roll
- Fruit

Provençal Vegetable Tian

4–6 SERVINGS

A tian is a casserole of summer vegetables that is cooked slowly for a long time. It takes about 3 hours to cook, so it's not something you want to make in the morning. Make it in advance on a slow weekend and set some aside for your bento during the week. It is delicious eaten hot, and even better when cold, so it's a great centerpiece for a warm-weather bento. The key to a great tian is to cook the vegetables until they are on the verge of becoming caramelized.

These recipe quantities are for a 10 x 12 inch (25 x 30cm) square, or 12 inch (30cm) diameter casserole dish.

¼ cup (60ml) olive oil, for sautéing
4 medium onions, thinly sliced
salt, for sprinkling
1 large eggplant, cut in half lengthwise and thinly sliced
2 medium zucchini, thinly sliced into rounds
4 large ripe tomatoes, de-seeded and chopped finely
black pepper, to taste
2 tsp fresh or 1 tsp dried thyme
¼ cup (60ml) olive oil, for drizzling

In a large frying pan, heat ¼ cup (60ml) of olive oil over medium-low heat. Add the onions and sprinkle on some salt (this helps to draw out the moisture so that the onions cook faster). Slowly sauté the onions over medium-low heat until they are translucent.

Sprinkle the eggplant with salt and massage the salt into the slices with your hands. Put in a colander to drain. Squeeze out any excess moisture.

Preheat the oven to 325°F (165°C).

Put the sliced zucchini in a single layer on a clean kitchen towel. Sprinkle lightly with salt, and leave for a few minutes to let the salt draw out some of the excess moisture. Pat dry.

Place a layer of cooked onions in a casserole dish, then a layer each of eggplant, zucchini, and tomato, adding a little black pepper and thyme to each layer. Repeat until all the vegetables are used up, finishing with a layer of tomato and a light sprinkle of salt. Drizzle on the remaining ¼ cup (60ml) of olive oil.

Bake for 1 hour uncovered, then cover with aluminum foil and bake for another 90 minutes, until the casserole is dark and concentrated and almost sticky.

AHEAD-OF-TIME NOTE: *Definitely something to make ahead, this can be stored in the refrigerator for up to a week. It also freezes very well.*

Beet Salad with Grainy Mustard Dressing

4 SERVINGS

So many people are afraid of using beets in salads, perhaps because of their bright purple color! So was I, until I came across a version of this sweet, tangy salad at a cooking class conducted by chef Erick Vedel in Arles, the town in France where Van Gogh went for inspiration. My version adds more spices to the dressing, which complements the earthy sweetness of the beet. This is absolutely delicious when eaten together with tender baby salad leaves.

3 cooked beets (precooked vacuum-packed or good quality canned beets are fine, but not pickled beets)
3 Tbsp grainy Dijon-style mustard
1 tsp ground cumin
1 tsp ground coriander
½ tsp sweet paprika
½ tsp ground cardamom
black pepper, to taste
1 Tbsp olive oil
1 tsp lemon juice
1 small red radish, sliced, for decoration

If you need to cook raw beets, cut off the leaves and wash off any dirt from the roots—don't peel or cut them at this point. Wrap each beet separately in aluminum foil and bake in the oven at 350°F (175°C) for 30 minutes, until tender. Peel when cooled. Cooked beets can be stored in a plastic bag in the refrigerator for 2–3 days.

If using canned beets, drain well before using. I recommend vacuum-packed precooked beets over canned, if you can get them—they have better flavor and texture.

Cut the beets into halves or quarters, then into ¼ inch (0.5cm) thick slices.

Place the mustard, spices, black pepper, oil, and lemon juice in a bowl, and whisk vigorously until combined. Taste, and adjust the seasoning. Mix in the beets. Place a portion of the salad in a small container that fits inside your bento box.

Create a "radish flower" decoration by arranging thinly sliced radish rounds in a flower shape on top of the salad.

This can be made up to 3 days in advance and held in the refrigerator.

TO PACK THIS BENTO

I've used a two-tier bento box with fairly deep (2 inch [5cm]) containers. One container holds a small individual ramekin with the tian, surrounded by lots of baby salad leaves. The other container is lined with more baby salad leaves, upon which a cup of the beet salad, another cup of fruit (grapes in this case, but use whatever is in season), and the cheeses rest. The important thing here is to keep the individual flavors separate until you are ready to eat. A crusty roll completes this mouthwatering lunch. Whether or not to have a glass of wine is entirely up to you!

TIMELINE

No timeline, since this is a make-ahead-and-refrigerate type of bento. Grab and go in the morning.

Real Cheese for Lunch!

Cheese for lunch is nothing new, but many people limit themselves to tiny prepackaged cheeses, or plastic-wrapped (and plastic-tasting) sliced, processed cheese for lunch. I think this is a shame. Cheese doesn't need to be kept ice cold all the time; true cheese connoisseurs take it out well in advance of eating so that it has a chance to come to room temperature, when it tastes the best. Be adventurous, and try small chunks of different cheeses in your bento boxes, wrapped in plastic wrap or freezer paper. If you have a good cheese shop in your neighborhood, get friendly with the cheesemonger.

Incidentally, I never use low-fat cheese. Real cheese to me is a special treat to be savored. There are some naturally low-fat cheeses, but industrially produced low-fat cheese is a rubbery, tasteless shadow of the real thing. I would much rather have a small quantity of the real thing than a low-fat version. Life is too short to waste on substandard food!

VARIATION RECIPES

Casserole Dishes

Casserole dishes work well in bentos. Think of the ones that taste great cold or reheated in the microwave, and set aside some on purpose—I call these "planned leftovers." Some ideas include: macaroni and cheese; gratin dishes; ratatouille; lasagna; and even tuna casserole, perhaps with a little extra cheese on top.

To freeze planned leftovers of casserole dishes, pack in individual portions. Suitable containers include neatly folded boxes of aluminum foil (which do have the disadvantage of not being microwaveable); small, sturdy, ovenproof glass or ceramic ramekins; or silicone cupcake liners. Wrap the leftovers well in foil or plastic wrap, then put into freezer-safe bags or plastic containers before freezing. Transfer to the refrigerator the night before you intend to use them, or defrost in the microwave (removing any foil beforehand) or in a regular oven.

I like to put a glass or ceramic container directly into a bento box, cushioned with other food such as salad greens, bread, or rice, to minimize the chance of breakage.

Baked Leftover Pasta

This is not a recipe per se, but a way to make leftover pasta taste like a treat instead of just leftovers.

If the pasta is plain, add a little sauce to it; if it's already sauced, you can use it as is or add a little extra leftover sauce if you have it. Put the pasta in a silicone baking cup or small ovenproof container. Top with a tablespoon of cream, a teaspoon of shredded cheese, and a sprinkle of dried oregano or thyme. Bake in a toaster oven until the cheese has melted and is lightly browned.

Leftover lasagna can be put into a baking cup or container and baked without any additions until bubbly and browned on top.

Broccoli and Ham Mini-casserole with Sour Cream

1 SERVING

You don't need to wait for leftovers to add a casserole dish to your bento. These individually sized mini-casseroles are easy to make in a toaster oven. If using a conventional oven, consider making several at once and freezing the extras.

1–2 cooked broccoli spears, roughly chopped
1 Tbsp chopped cooked ham
1 Tbsp finely chopped onion
½ tsp butter
salt and pepper, to taste
3 Tbsp sour cream or crème fraîche
pinch dried thyme

Sauté the broccoli, ham, and onion in the butter in a small frying pan over medium heat until the onion is translucent. Season with salt and pepper. Remove from the heat and place in a silicone baking cup or small ovenproof container.

In a small bowl, combine the cream and salt and pepper and pour over the broccoli and ham. Sprinkle with dried thyme. Bake in a toaster oven at 400°F (200°C) for 8–10 minutes, until bubbly. Let cool to room temperature before packing into a bento box.

Fennel, Tomato, and Scallop Mini-casserole

1 SERVING

½ small fennel bulb, finely sliced
½ tsp olive oil
1 fresh or frozen scallop, cut into quarters
1 whole canned tomato, drained and chopped
pinch herbes de Provence
salt and pepper, to taste

In a small frying pan, sauté the fennel in the olive oil over high heat until softened. Add the scallop and sauté for a few seconds. Add the tomato and simmer for a minute. Season with herbes de Provence, salt, and pepper.

Put into a silicone baking cup or small ovenproof container. Sprinkle with the herbs.

Bake in a toaster oven at 400°F (200°C) for 8–10 minutes until bubbly. Let cool to room temperature before packing into a bento box.

VARIATION: *Use 2 or 3 small shrimps, whole or chopped, instead of the scallop.*

Spanish Omelette Bento

This potato-and-vegetable-filled cold omelette is a great picnic or bento item. To go with this is an equally hearty vegetable dish: braised savory-sweet broccoli rabe with garlic and dried fruit.

Spanish Omelette with Potato, Onion, and Sweet Pepper

2 SERVINGS (1 OMELETTE)

The Spanish members of the Just Bento web site community are passionate about "tortilla"—not the corn or wheat flatbread Mexican variety, but the thick, savory, potato-filled omelette that is considered one of the national dishes of Spain. I hope they will forgive me for adding some diced sweet pepper and onion to the classic recipe.

2 medium potatoes
2 Tbsp olive oil
salt, for sprinkling
½ small onion finely chopped
½ medium red sweet pepper, de-seeded and cut into small dice
black pepper, to taste
4 large eggs
½ tsp salt
salad greens to line the bento

Peel the potatoes and slice as thinly as possible. A mandoline or plastic vegetable slicer is the handiest tool for this.

Heat 1 tablespoon of the olive oil in a 7–8 inch (18–20cm) nonstick frying pan over medium heat. Put in the potato slices, add a sprinkle of salt, and sauté until the potato starts to turn limp. Add the onion and sweet red pepper, and continue to sauté until both have softened. Season with a little more salt and pepper. Remove the vegetables from the pan and set aside.

Beat the eggs well with the ½ teaspoon of salt and a few grinds of pepper. Put the remaining 1 tablespoon of olive oil into the same pan and turn the heat up to high. Pour the beaten egg into the hot pan and then add the potatoes, onion, and sweet pepper. Turn the

heat immediately to low and cook for 10–15 minutes, until the top is almost set.

Take a plate or a second frying pan and flip the omelette upside down on it. (If you are brave, try flipping it in the air!) Slip the upside-down omelette back in the pan and cook for 3–4 more minutes. Let cool completely. Cut into wedges and arrange on a bed of salad greens.

VARIATIONS: *Add a little chopped and precooked ham or bacon, chopped leftover cooked vegetables or meat, cheese, and so on.*

AHEAD-OF-TIME NOTE: *You can make this up to a couple of days before, and store it in the refrigerator. It does not freeze well, since the potato texture turns unpleasantly grainy when frozen.*

Broccoli Rabe with Garlic and Dried Fruit

1 SERVING

Broccoli rabe, also known as rapini or sprouting broccoli, is a dark green, vigorous version of regular broccoli. If you can't find it, use regular broccoli instead. This winter dish is salty yet sweet, a flavor combination that I love. It's also full of vitamins and fiber.

½ Tbsp olive oil
2 garlic cloves, peeled and thinly sliced
2 cups (80g) roughly chopped broccoli rabe
½ cup (120ml) water
1 Tbsp red wine vinegar
½ Tbsp raisins
½ Tbsp dried cranberries
salt and pepper, to taste

Heat the oil in a large frying pan over medium heat, add the garlic, and sauté until softened. Add the broccoli rabe and sauté briefly. Add the water, vinegar, and dried fruit and bring to a boil. Season with salt and pepper. Turn the heat to medium-low and simmer until the liquid has evaporated, turning the broccoli occasionally with a spatula. Taste and adjust the seasonings.

VARIATION: *Try red currants or golden raisins as the dried fruit, or even finely chopped prunes. The savory-sweet combination also works with cabbage, kale, and collard greens; if using the latter two, blanch briefly in boiling water before sautéing.*

TO PACK THIS BENTO

Pack the broccoli rabe into a small container and seasonal fruit of your choice into a small cup—here I've used some clementine orange segments. Cut the omelette in half, and the half into wedges. Put the box of broccoli rabe and the fruit cup inside the main bento box (you can carry these separately in side boxes if you prefer). Arrange some salad greens in the rest of the main box and put the omelette wedges on top.

TIMELINE

Both the omelette and the broccoli rabe dish can be made the night before; just pack it up in the morning with the salad greens and fruit.

VARIATION RECIPES
Bento-friendly Egg Dishes

When the refrigerator seems to be empty, and there's a corner of your bento to fill, eggs are a great fallback. While tamagoyaki (see page 19) is a bento staple, here are some of the many other ways I use eggs.

Scrambled Eggs with Sofrito
1 SERVING

Sofrito is a mixture of various aromatic vegetables that is a staple in Mexican cooking. This scrambled-egg dish is great with bread or rice.

1 large egg
salt and pepper, to taste
pinch red chili flakes, optional
1 tsp olive oil
1 Tbsp homemade or store-bought sofrito (see below)

Beat the egg with the salt and pepper, and the chili flakes if desired. Heat the oil in a small frying pan over high heat. Add the sofrito and the egg and stir rapidly for 3–4 minutes until crumbly. Let cool completely before packing into a bento box.

Sofrito
MAKES 4 CUPS (800G)

I usually have a jar of sofrito on hand. I add it to eggs, sautéed vegetables, stir-fried rice, and many

other bento dishes. Sofrito keeps in the refrigerator for a couple of weeks, and can also be frozen. Sofrito can be cooked or uncooked; I prefer mine cooked, since I think the sautéing brings out the flavors better. There's a lot of chopping involved, so a food processor comes in handy. You can buy ready-made sofrito, but making it yourself is so much better.

2 large ripe tomatoes
3 Tbsp olive or vegetable oil
2 medium green sweet peppers, de-seeded and finely chopped
2 medium red sweet peppers, de-seeded and finely chopped
1 large onion, finely chopped
6 large garlic cloves, finely minced
½ cup (10g) chopped fresh coriander leaves
½ cup (10g) chopped flat leaf parsley

Bring a pot of water to a boil. Dunk the tomatoes in the water for a minute, then take them out and cool them under running water. Peel the tomatoes and chop roughly.

Heat the oil in a large frying pan over medium-high heat. Add the sweet peppers, onion, and garlic. Sauté until the onion is translucent and the vegetables smell very aromatic. Add the tomato, coriander, and parsley, and sauté for 3–4 minutes. Remove from the heat and let cool.

Store the sofrito in a glass or ceramic container rather than a plastic one, since the odors of the garlic and onion will permeate the plastic permanently. An empty jam jar is perfect.

Fresh Herb and Cream Cheese Omelette
1 SERVING

The cheese adds a creamy-tangy flavor to this omelette, which is good cold or warm.

1 large egg
1 Tbsp finely chopped fresh parsley
1 Tbsp finely chopped fresh chives
salt and pepper, to taste
2 tsp olive oil
1 Tbsp cream cheese, in small chunks

Beat the egg together with the herbs. Season with salt and pepper and mix again.

Heat the oil in a small nonstick frying pan over high heat. Pour in the egg mixture, and cook while stirring gently until the egg is almost set. Scatter the cream cheese on the surface.

Fold the omelette in half, and then half again, to form a quarter-round shape. Press down firmly with a spatula. Remove from the pan and cut in half. Let cool completely before packing into a bento box.

Omelette with Kimchi and Ham

1 SERVING

This is tasty with or without the ham—or try some chopped shrimp instead. Go easy on the salt, since kimchi is already quite salty.

1 large egg
salt and pepper, to taste
1 tsp vegetable oil
2 Tbsp well-drained and finely chopped kimchi
1 Tbsp chopped cooked ham

Beat the egg and season with the salt and pepper. Heat the oil in a small nonstick frying pan over high heat. Pour in the beaten egg and cook until almost set on the top. Arrange the kimchi and ham in the center of the egg and roll the egg over and around the filling. Flip over so the seam is on the bottom, and press. Remove from the pan and let cool completely before slicing and packing into a bento box.

Saucy Eggs

MAKES 4

These eggs are great with plain rice, or mashed and used as a sandwich filling.

4 eggs
½ medium onion, grated
½ cup (120ml) ketchup
¼ cup (60ml) Worcestershire sauce
¼ cup (60ml) water

Boil the eggs for 6 minutes so that they are soft boiled, but not runny. Combine all of the ingredients in a pan except for the eggs. Place the pan over medium heat until the sauce is bubbling slowly. Peel and add the eggs and simmer for 5 minutes, turning the eggs frequently. Drain off most of the sauce before packing into a bento box.

Soft-boiled Egg in a Cup with Sofrito

1 SERVING

Here's another sofrito-egg recipe—almost the exact same ingredients as for the scrambled eggs above—but a very different texture.

1 egg
1 Tbsp Sofrito (see facing page)
salt and pepper, to taste

Boil the egg for 3 minutes so that it is soft and runny. Peel and mash roughly with a fork. Mix with the sofrito

and season with a little salt and pepper. Mound the egg-and-sofrito mixture into a silicone baking cup. Microwave on high for 1 minute. The egg should still be soft and wobbly when you poke it.

Soy-sauce Eggs

1 SERVING

These appeared regularly in the bentos my mother made for me when I was growing up.

1 Tbsp soy sauce
1 hard-boiled egg (see page 60), peeled

Heat the soy sauce in a small pan over medium heat. Add the hard-boiled egg and roll it around in the soy sauce until it is a burnished brown on the outside. Let cool, then cut into halves or quarters.

Miso-marinated Eggs

1 SERVING

This recipe is one of the most popular on the Just Bento web site. The sweetened miso permeates the egg, giving it a wonderful savory flavor.

1 Tbsp white miso
1–2 tsp maple syrup, honey, or brown sugar
1 hard-boiled egg (see page 60), peeled

Put the miso and sweetener in the center of a piece of plastic wrap. Gather the ends of the plastic wrap up to make a pouch, and squish the pouch several times to mix the miso and sweetener together. Unwrap the plastic, and place the hard-boiled egg in the middle. Wrap the plastic around the egg, encasing it in the miso mixture. Place the wrapped egg in a bowl or a plastic bag and leave in the refrigerator for at least 5 hours or up to a week.

When ready to use, remove from the plastic wrap and wipe the miso away with a paper towel.

Deviled Eggs

1 SERVING

1 hard-boiled egg (see page 60), peeled
mayonnaise, to taste

Cut the egg in half and remove the egg yolk. Mix with enough mayonnaise to make a paste. Mound the paste back into the egg-white halves.

There are endless ways to vary deviled eggs. You can add chopped parsley, a little sweet paprika, capers, chopped pickle, drained and flaked canned tuna, finely chopped ham, and so on.

Quinoa Pilau and Chickpea Salad Bento

Even though I'm an omnivore, I like to get my protein from many sources instead of just relying on meat or fish. This bento uses several different protein-rich foods that are combined to make a nutritious, filling, and above all delicious meal. It has a spicy pilau made with quinoa (a seed that is used in recipes as a grain, and is very high in protein) and flavored with a little bacon, and a chickpea salad with feta cheese. Both of these dishes could be prepared for dinner, with some set aside for a bento in the next day or so—what I call "planned leftovers."

CONTENTS

- Spicy Quinoa Pilau with Bacon
- Mediterranean Chickpea Salad with Feta Cheese

Spicy Quinoa Pilau with Bacon

4 SERVINGS

I don't know why interesting grains are all too often reserved for vegetarians and dieters. Quinoa is not only very nutritious, it has an interesting texture, and is a nice change from rice-based bentos.

1 cup (170g) uncooked quinoa
1 Tbsp olive oil
1½ oz (50g) Canadian-style bacon or gammon, cut into small dice
½ small onion, chopped (Tip: use half a red onion here and reserve the rest for the salad)
1 garlic clove, peeled and finely chopped
½ yellow sweet pepper, de-seeded and finely chopped
2 cups (480ml) vegetable or chicken stock
1 bay leaf
½ tsp ground allspice
½ small zucchini, cut in half lengthwise and thinly sliced into rounds
1 cup (130g) chopped leftover cooked vegetables of your choice
salt and pepper, to taste
½ to 1 tsp harissa or other hot red chili paste, to taste

Rinse the quinoa in cold water and drain well in a fine-mesh colander.

Heat the olive oil in a large frying pan over high heat. Add the bacon and sauté until the bacon starts to change color. Add the onion, garlic, and yellow sweet pepper. Add the quinoa and sauté until the seeds start to brown.

Add the stock and bring to a boil. Put in the bay leaf, allspice, zucchini, and chopped vegetables. Lower the heat and simmer for 15–20 minutes, until the liquid has just about evaporated. Season with the salt and pepper.

Turn off the heat and cover. Let stand for a few minutes until the quinoa has absorbed any remaining liquid. Stir in the harissa or red chili paste.

This pilau is delicious hot or cold. Leftovers keep in the refrigerator for 2–3 days.

TIP: *If you can't get hold of quinoa, millet works well in this recipe.*

Mediterranean Chickpea Salad with Feta Cheese

2 SERVINGS

This salty-sour, crunchy salad is my own variation on a standard side dish at one of my favorite Greek diners in Long Island, New York.

15 oz (425g) can chickpeas, drained and rinsed
6–8 cherry tomatoes, cut into quarters
¼ cup (40g) finely chopped red onion
¼ cup (7g) roughly chopped flat leaf parsley, leaves only
1 Tbsp capers
2 Tbsp lemon juice
1 Tbsp olive oil
pinch salt
black pepper, to taste
2 oz (60g) feta cheese, cut into small cubes

Combine all of the ingredients in a bowl. Mix well and let marinate in the refrigerator overnight. This salad can be kept in the refrigerator, stored in a tightly sealed container, for 3–4 days.

TO PACK THIS BENTO

The pilau and salad should be kept separate until lunchtime, so a two-tier or two-section box is recommended for this bento. Here, I've used two nesting plastic bento boxes. The smaller box, which contains the salad, can be stored neatly inside the large box when empty, taking up less space on the trip home.

TIMELINE

As mentioned above, both recipes can be made a day or more ahead and stored in the refrigerator. The pilau can be frozen for up to a month in advance.

Whole Grains and Dried Beans

Including whole grains and beans in your bentos is a great way to add fiber, vitamins, and minerals to your diet, not to mention a lot of interesting textures and flavors. Whole grains and dried beans can be divided into two groups: types that can be cooked in under 45 minutes, and types that need a lot longer.

Whole grains and legumes that can be cooked in less than 45 minutes include lentils, quinoa, millet, and amaranth. Split, smashed, parboiled, or otherwise pre-processed grains and legumes such as cracked wheat and rolled oatmeal also fall into this category. All other whole grains and legumes need to be soaked in water for several hours before cooking.

If you eat a lot of beans and grains, a pressure cooker is a great investment. A pressure cooker makes it possible to cook almost any type of bean or grain in under 30 minutes. In a regular pan, for instance, it takes 3–4 hours to cook soybeans until they are soft, but in a pressure cooker it takes just half an hour.

The recipes below are all made with beans and grains that cook quickly. They are of course all delicious when eaten cold, and can all be made in advance—two important criteria for anything going into a bento box.

Stewed Lentils with Fresh Herbs

6 SERVINGS

Be sure to use firm, unhulled green lentils rather than brown, yellow, or red lentils—the latter varieties will disintegrate into mush.

1 cup (190g) uncooked firm green lentils, such as Puy lentils
1 Tbsp olive oil
1 small onion, finely chopped
½ celery stalk, finely chopped
1 small carrot, finely chopped
1 cup (240ml) chicken or vegetable stock
1 garlic clove, finely chopped
1 tsp dried thyme
1 bay leaf
salt and pepper, to taste
chopped fresh herbs, such as parsley, chervil, or chives, to taste
lemon wedge, optional

Rinse the lentils. Put into a pot and add enough water to come up to 1 inch (2.5cm) above the surface of the lentils. Bring to a boil over high heat, then turn the heat to medium-low and simmer for 15 minutes, or until the lentils are cooked through but still firm. Drain the lentils into a colander. Rinse out the pot and dry.

Add oil to the pot. Over high heat, sauté the onion, celery, carrot, and garlic until softened. Add the cooked lentils, stock, thyme, and bay leaf. Bring to a boil, then turn the heat to low and simmer until the moisture is almost gone. Season with salt and pepper and remove from the heat. Take out the bay leaf.

This dish keeps refrigerated for up to a week. Mix with a generous quantity of chopped fresh herbs before packing, and add a wedge of lemon.

Millet and Potato Pancakes

MAKES 12–14 SMALL PANCAKES

Millet is a tiny, round grain. There are many varieties available, but the type you see most often at health food stores and some supermarkets is pearl millet, which works well in this recipe.

These moist little pancakes contain both cooked, fluffy millet and crunchy toasted millet, and are great hot out of the pan or cold.

3½ oz (100g) uncooked millet
1 cup (240ml) water
1 Tbsp uncooked millet
1 egg
¼ cup (60ml) buttermilk
½ cup (100g) cooked, cold mashed potato
3 Tbsp all-purpose flour
½ tsp salt
vegetable oil or butter, for frying

Combine the 3½ oz (100g) millet and the water in a small pan. Bring to a boil, then lower the heat and simmer until the moisture is almost gone and the millet is light and fluffy.

In the meantime, put the tablespoon of millet in a small dry frying pan over high heat. Dry-roast until the millet is very lightly browned. Remove from the pan and leave to cool.

Beat the egg and buttermilk together. Add the boiled millet, mashed potato, flour, and salt. Stir in the toasted millet. Add a little more buttermilk if the batter seems too thick.

Heat the oil or butter in a large nonstick frying pan over medium-high heat. Drop tablespoons of the batter onto the hot surface and cook for about 3 minutes on one side, and 2–3 minutes on the other side.

Pack these pancakes with a soup or stew bento, or use like sandwich bread.

Amaranth Dip

MAKES 2 CUPS (500G)

Like quinoa, amaranth is actually a seed that is used like a grain, and is a very good source of protein. When cooked, amaranth has a rather sticky, viscous texture that people either love or hate. I happen to love it, especially in this spicy dip. Use the dip for raw vegetable sticks or on flatbreads. Use whole-grain amaranth, not the flaked kind sold as breakfast cereal.

1 cup (190g) uncooked whole-grain amaranth
2 Tbsp olive oil
1 small onion, finely chopped
1 inch (2.5cm) piece fresh ginger, peeled and finely chopped
1 garlic clove, finely chopped
3 cups (720ml) water
1 tsp salt
1 tsp ground cumin
1 tsp ground coriander
½ tsp black pepper
1–2 Tbsp harissa or other red chili paste

Place the amaranth in a large dry frying pan over high heat. Stir and dry-roast until the grains are light brown in color. Remove from the heat.

Heat 1 tablespoon of the olive oil in a heavy-bottomed pan over medium heat and add the onion, ginger, and garlic. Sauté until softened. Add the amaranth, water, and salt. Bring to a boil, add the dry spices, then lower the heat to a simmer. Cook, stirring occasionally to prevent the amaranth from sticking to the bottom of the pan, until the amaranth has a runny, pastelike consistency. Add the harissa and the remaining olive oil. Taste, and adjust the seasonings. This keeps in the refrigerator for 3–4 days.

Bulgur Wheat with Roasted Garlic and Pine Nuts

1 SERVING

Bulgur wheat is whole wheat that is parboiled and processed. It is best known as the key ingredient in tabbouleh, a Middle Eastern salad, but it can be used in many other ways too. It needs almost no cooking to become soft enough to eat while still retaining its crunchy texture.

¼ cup (35g) uncooked bulgur wheat
1 cup (240ml) boiling water
1 Tbsp pine nuts
2 cloves Roasted Garlic (see page 88), squeezed out of the skins and mashed
salt and pepper, to taste

Put the bulgur wheat in a microwave-safe container. Cover with the boiling water. Microwave on high for 2 minutes, then let stand for 5 minutes. (If you don't have a microwave, leave the bulgur wheat and water tightly covered for 15 minutes.)

Heat a small frying pan over high heat and add the pine nuts. Stir and dry-roast until the nuts are turning brown and smell toasty. Remove from the heat.

Combine the bulgur wheat, roasted garlic, and pine nuts. Season with the salt and pepper.

Soup and Muffin Bento

Hot soup is always comforting on a cold day. By using a thermal lunch jar, you can have piping-hot soup even without access to a microwave. The chicken and vegetable soup is paired here with savory muffins and warm stewed apples for a very satisfying meal. Everything is made in advance, and simply heated up in the morning.

CONTENTS

Leftover Roast Chicken and Vegetable Soup

6 SERVINGS

This is another example of what I call "planned leftovers." Set aside some meat as well as the carcass from a roast chicken to make this hearty soup. Add some cubed potato, short pasta, noodles, canned beans, or rice to make it even heartier.

roast chicken carcass from the day before, plus any pan juices
2 celery stalks, leaves reserved
handful parsley for the stock, plus more parsley for garnish
1 bay leaf
1 medium onion
2 medium carrots
1 Tbsp olive oil
2 cups (280g) chopped roast chicken meat
15 oz (425g) can crushed tomatoes
1 tsp dried thyme
1 chicken stock cube, optional
salt and pepper, to taste

Put the roast chicken carcass and pan juices into a pot with the celery leaves, parsley, and bay leaf. Add enough water to cover. Bring to a gentle boil, then lower the heat and simmer gently for 20 minutes.

In the meantime, chop up the onion, celery stalks, and carrots, and sauté in the olive oil in a heavy-bottomed pot.

Strain the stock made from the chicken carcass through a colander into the pot with the sautéed vegetables. Add the canned tomatoes. Simmer for at least another 10–15 minutes, or longer for a deeper flavor.

Add the chopped chicken meat and thyme; add a chicken stock cube for even more flavor. Season with salt (not too much if you are using the stock cube) and pepper. The parsley garnish can be packed separately and sprinkled on just before you eat the soup.

Edamame and Cheese Muffins

MAKES 10–12

I am not too fond of sweet muffins—to me they seem rather like cupcakes that didn't quite make the grade. But I do love savory muffins like these edamame-and-cheese ones. They're great for lunch and snacks, and are a nice accompaniment to the soup.

Basic savory muffin batter
2 large eggs
⅔ cup (160ml) milk
¼ cup (60ml) olive oil
2 cups (250g) cake flour or all-purpose flour
1 tsp baking powder
1 tsp salt

Additions
2½ oz (70g) cheddar cheese, shredded
4 Tbsp frozen or fresh shelled edamame beans

Preheat the oven to 350°F (180°C).

In a small bowl, beat the eggs with a whisk until foamy. Add the milk and olive oil and mix well.

Sift together the flour, baking powder, and salt, and add to the wet ingredients little by little until it is all incorporated. Add half the cheese and mix well. If the batter seems too thick, add a little more milk.

Pour the batter into nonstick or silicone-lined muffin cups. The muffin cups should each be half full of batter. Put a few edamame in each cup. Fresh edamame should be blanched first; frozen edamame can be put directly into the batter. Sprinkle the rest of the cheese on top. Bake for 20–25 minutes, until golden brown on top.

TIP: *Using cake flour will result in lighter, fluffier muffins. Muffins made with all-purpose flour will be denser, though still very good.*

AHEAD-OF-TIME NOTE: *These muffins freeze very successfully. Line up on a plate or baking sheet individually and freeze. Put the frozen muffins in freezer bags or containers. They keep for about a month.*

MUFFIN VARIATIONS

Try adding these ingredients to the basic savory muffin batter on page 103 instead of the edamame and cheddar cheese:

- Cooked ham and shredded Gruyère cheese
- Chopped parsley and crispy cooked bacon bits
- Frozen peas and carrots and grated Parmesan cheese
- Dried herbs
- ¼ cup (15g) finely chopped sun-dried tomatoes and 2 Tbsp chopped black olives
- ½ cup (45g) sautéed onion and grated Parmesan cheese

Also try replacing the olive oil in the basic savory muffin batter with:

- ¼ cup (60ml) homemade or store-bought basil pesto sauce
- ¼ cup (60ml) melted butter. This variation is not the healthiest, perhaps, but oh so good!
- ¼ cup (60ml) canola or other flavorless oil, for light-tasting muffins

Warm Apple Compote

2–4 SERVINGS

Apple wedges are simmered in a honey-lemon mix until tender to make a delicious dessert. Use sweet eating apples for this, not sour cooking apples. It is equally good warm or cold.

1 lemon	¼ tsp cinnamon
2 apples	3 Tbsp honey

Remove just the yellow outer peel of the lemon with a sharp knife, leaving the white, bitter pith behind. Juice the lemon.

Peel and cut the apples into wedges. Put in a pan with just enough water to cover, and add the lemon juice and peel, cinnamon, and honey. Bring to a boil, then lower the heat and simmer gently for about twenty minutes until the apple wedges are soft and semi-translucent. Let cool in the poaching liquid.

This dish can be kept in the refrigerator for up to a week, with the apple wedges immersed in the poaching liquid.

TO PACK THIS BENTO IN A THERMAL LUNCH JAR

Using a thermal lunch jar will keep this bento warm until lunchtime. Reheat the muffins in the microwave or toaster oven and pack them in the largest thermal container of the lunch jar while still warm. (I find that I can fit two muffins in the largest container of an adult-sized thermal lunch jar). Reheat the soup until piping hot and put into the soup container with the leakproof lid. Reheat the Apple Compote if you wish to eat it warm, and put in a third container. See Bento Boxes and Accessories (page 114) for more about thermal lunch jars and how they work.

If you don't have a thermal lunch jar and have no access to a microwave oven at lunchtime, try packing the soup in an insulated mug.

TIMELINE

MINUTES	10	5	0
Soup	☑ reheat soup until piping hot	☑ put soup into insulated container	
Muffins and Compote	☑ heat up muffins in toaster oven (5 min) or microwave (2 min)	☑ pack compote in container	☑ pack muffins in insulated container
Thermal lunch jar prep and packing	☑ boil water in electric kettle or on stove top	☑ pour out boiling water, wipe containers	☑ pack inner containers into outer container, put in insulating bag
		☑ pour boiling water into containers, leave for 2 minutes	

Make in advance: Muffins. Soup. Apple Compote.

Prep the night before: Transfer frozen components to refrigerator to defrost.

Thermal Lunch Jar–friendly Dishes

Thermal lunch jars may seem like the perfect solution to the "I want to bring my lunch, but I want it warm" dilemma. However, they aren't suitable for all foods. Keep in mind that a thermal lunch jar keeps food warm for several hours, during which time the food continues to cook. Think of them as small, portable steam tables, the kind you see at buffets. Food that just needs to be cooked for a short time before eating will suffer. On the other hand, any kind of stew or soup will get even better. Here are some recipes that are great in thermal lunch jars.

Portable Chicken Pot Pie

2 SERVINGS

This is a great way to use up day-old croissants, as well as leftover roast chicken. The croissant is used instead of a piecrust and packed separately. The stew tastes better when made a day in advance, and can be frozen for up to a month.

½ cup (120ml) chicken stock	2 oz (60g) cooked chicken,
1 Tbsp butter	roughly chopped
½ small onion, roughly chopped	2 Tbsp frozen green peas
½ small carrot, roughly chopped	1 Tbsp heavy cream
1 inch (2.5cm) length celery	pinch dried thyme
stalk, roughly chopped	salt and pepper, to taste
2 Tbsp flour	1 croissant per bento
½ cup (120ml) whole milk	

Heat the chicken stock in a small pan. Heat the butter in a large frying pan over medium-high heat. Add the onion, carrot, and celery, and sauté until softened. Add the flour, and stir until the flour coats the vegetables.

Add the hot chicken stock to the frying pan, stirring rapidly. Add the milk. Add the chicken and the peas and simmer for a few minutes until the stew is slightly thickened. Add the cream and the thyme and season with salt and pepper. Simmer for 4–5 minutes more. Pack a single portion (about half this quantity) into a prepared thermal lunch jar while piping hot.

If the croissant is stale, put it in the oven or toaster oven for a few minutes until crispy. Let cool completely. Pack separately. At lunchtime, put the croissant on top of the stew and let sit for a few minutes before eating.

Deconstructed Wonton Soup

1 SERVING

I love the taste of wonton soup, but it can be a bother to form the wonton dumplings. This is a quick version that tastes just as good.

½ cup (120ml) chicken stock	½ tsp sesame oil
2 Tbsp ground pork	4–5 wonton wrappers, cut into
½ tsp peeled and grated fresh	thirds
ginger	salt and pepper, to taste
½ tsp grated onion	1 Tbsp chopped green onion
½ tsp soy sauce	

Heat the chicken stock in a small pan. In a bowl, mix together the pork, ginger, grated onion, soy sauce, and sesame oil. Form the mixture into small balls and drop into the hot chicken stock. Simmer for 4–5 minutes.

Add the wonton wrappers and simmer for another minute. Taste, and season with salt and pepper. Sprinkle the green onion on top and pack into a prepared thermal lunch jar while piping hot.

Pork and Jalapeño Chili

8 SERVINGS

Any kind of chili is perfect for a thermal lunch jar. This mildly spicy pork and jalapeño chili goes well with a slightly sweet corn muffin or cornbread; you can also bring along some plain rice, hominy, or boiled potatoes. It is best made in some quantity, so make it for dinner and hold back some for a bento the next day.

1 Tbsp vegetable oil	7 oz (200g) jar pickled, sliced
8 oz (225g) pork shoulder, cut	jalapeños
into ½ inch (1cm) cubes	3 cups (720ml) chicken stock
1 medium onion, chopped	15 oz (425g) can crushed
1 green sweet pepper, de-seeded	tomatoes
and chopped	1 Tbsp ground cumin
1 celery stalk, chopped	salt and pepper, to taste
4 garlic cloves, finely chopped	

Heat the vegetable oil in a heavy-bottomed pan over high heat. Add the pork and brown. Remove the pork from the pan and put in the onion, green pepper, celery, and garlic. Sauté until softened.

Put the whole jar of jalapeños, pickling liquid and all, into a food processor. Process until finely chopped. If you don't have a food processor, drain the jalapeños, reserving the liquid, and chop them finely with a knife.

Put the chopped jalapeños and liquid, chicken stock, tomatoes, and cumin into the pot. Bring to a boil, then lower the heat and add the browned pork. Turn the heat to medium-low and simmer for 30–40 minutes until the pork is very soft. Taste, and season with salt and pepper. (Be sure to taste before adding salt, since the jalapeño liquid is already quite salty.) This dish can also be made in a slow cooker.

Everyone Loves A Pie Bento

Everyone loves a pie, right? I do! There are all kinds of little portable pies or turnovers around the globe: Cornish pasties, the traditional miners' lunch in Cornwall, England; empanadas from Spain, Portugal, and South America; spicy Jamaican meat patties; and even the Italian calzone. My version has a yeasted, herbed whole wheat crust that can accommodate all kinds of savory fillings, even leftovers. I've given recipes for three different kinds of filling.

CONTENTS

- Savory Pies with Herbed Whole Wheat Crust
- Overnight Pickled Winter Vegetables

Savory Pies with Herbed Whole Wheat Crust

MAKES 8–10 PIES

The crust used here is yeasted dough made with whole wheat flour and olive oil. It's much easier to handle and healthier than a traditional pie crust made with butter, lard, or shortening. Try to roll it out thinly for the best texture.

I've included recipes for three pie fillings: a hearty yet quick-to-prepare mixture of canned corned beef and cabbage; a deeply flavored stewed beef and mushroom; and spinach with cheese.

A note about the flour: In the US, soft whole wheat flour works well in this recipe. If you can't get hold of this, use half whole wheat flour and half all-purpose white flour. In Europe, regular whole wheat flour works fine.

For the crust

1 tsp active dry yeast	1 tsp salt
½ tsp sugar	¼ cup (60ml) olive oil
2 cups (240g) whole wheat flour	¾ cup (180ml) warm water
1 tsp dried thyme or herbes de Provence	1 small egg
	1 tsp water

Dissolve the yeast and sugar in the warm water. Use a bowl large enough to allow for the liquid to foam up to 3 times its original volume. Leave in a warm place until foamy. (Tip: if it hasn't foamed up after about half an hour, you probably have old yeast; throw it out and try again with another packet.)

In a large bowl, mix together the flour, herbs, and salt. Add the olive oil. Add the water and the yeast-and-sugar mixture little by little, mixing with a wooden spoon. It will gradually form a shaggy ball. Add sprinkles of flour if the dough is too sticky. Knead the dough for a few minutes until smooth and pliable. Form into a smooth ball.

Put the dough into a large plastic ziplock bag and seal. If you are making the pies the same day, leave the dough in a warm place for an hour. If not, put it in the refrigerator overnight, where it will rise slowly.

When you are ready to make the pies, preheat the oven to 350°F (175°C). Beat the egg in a small bowl with a teaspoon of water.

Punch down the dough and divide into 8–10 pieces. Roll or flatten out the pieces into 7 inch (18cm) diameter circles. Place 3 heaping tablespoons of filling in the center of each circle, keeping a ½ inch (1cm) gap around the edges. Fold each circle of dough in half over the filling to form a pie, and crimp the edges firmly with a fork to seal. Brush the tops of the pies with the egg glaze.

Place the pies on a baking sheet that has been oiled or lined with a nonstick liner, and bake for 40–45 minutes until golden brown and puffy.

AHEAD-OF-TIME NOTE: *These pies can be frozen before or after baking. Bake uncooked, frozen pies straight from the freezer for 50–55 minutes. Defrost already-baked pies overnight in the refrigerator for the best flavor and texture.*

Corned Beef and Cabbage Filling

FILLS 8–10 PIES

1 Tbsp olive oil
½ small onion, finely sliced
2 cups (140g) shredded cabbage
3 oz (90g) canned corned beef
1 tsp ground cumin
salt and pepper, to taste

Heat the oil in a frying pan over high heat and sauté the onion until lightly browned. Add the cabbage and sauté until limp. Lower the heat to medium and crumble the corned beef into the pan. Mix to combine. Season with cumin, salt, and pepper. Let the filling cool to room temperature before using it to fill the pies. It can be made a day in advance and refrigerated.

Beef, Mushroom, and Guinness Filling

FILLS 8–10 PIES

½ small onion, finely sliced
1 Tbsp butter or olive oil
2 large or 4 medium mushrooms, finely sliced
8 oz (225g) beef sirloin, thinly sliced

1 Tbsp flour
½ cup (120ml) Guinness or other dark stout
1 Tbsp Worcestershire sauce
salt and pepper, to taste

Sauté the onion in the butter or oil until lightly browned. Add the mushrooms and sauté until browned. Add the beef and sauté until browned.

Add the flour and stir to coat the beef and onion. Add the Guinness or stout and the Worcestershire sauce. Stir until the gravy has thickened and is no longer runny. Season with salt and pepper. Let the filling cool to room temperature before using to fill the pies. It can be made a day in advance and refrigerated.

Spinach and Cheese Filling

FILLS 8–10 PIES

1 Tbsp olive oil
½ medium onion, thinly sliced
1 garlic clove, peeled and crushed
8 oz (225g) spinach leaves, washed and dried

salt and pepper, to taste
6 oz (170g) Gruyère cheese or similar strong, hard cheese, cut into ¼ inch (0.5cm) cubes

Heat the oil in a frying pan over high heat. Add the onion and sauté until lightly browned. Add the garlic and stir briefly. Add the spinach and sauté rapidly—the leaves will shrink down to a small mass. Season with a little salt (not too much, since the cheese is salty) and black pepper.

Turn the spinach out into a colander to drain away excess moisture. Let it cool to room temperature.

Fill the pies with a spoonful of spinach, and add some cheese cubes before sealing the edges. The spinach can still be rather moist even after draining, so take care that the moisture doesn't run over the edges of the dough, or the pies may open up during baking.

VARIATIONS: *Any kind of leftover meat, cooked vegetables, or even just some sautéed mushrooms with garlic make great pie fillings. If using something like leftover stew or curry, make sure the sauce is strained off or thickened enough so as not to run over the edges of the pie when filling it.*

You can also use this dough to make open-face mini-pies. Cut the dough into 6–12 pieces, flatten the pieces, and use each piece to line a muffin tin. Fill with the savory filling of your choice, top with some cheese, and bake at 350°F (175°C) for 40–45 minutes.

Overnight Pickled Winter Vegetables

MAKES 4 CUPS (600G)

This is a spicy, very easy-to-make winter salad that also has the advantage of being a good keeper in the refrigerator.

4–5 cauliflower florets
4–5 broccoli florets
1 cup (130g) halved and sliced carrot
1 cup (240ml) white wine vinegar
2 tsp sea salt
¼ cup (60ml) honey

1 Tbsp mustard seeds
2–3 cardamom pods
1 bay leaf
1 Tbsp whole black peppercorns
3 whole hot red dried chilies
1 cup (100g) celery stalk, cut into ½ inch (1cm) pieces

Blanch the cauliflower, broccoli, and carrot in boiling water for 3–5 minutes. Drain and let cool.

Combine the vinegar, salt, honey, and spices in a small pan. Bring to a boil while mixing to melt the honey. Remove from the heat and allow to cool a little.

Put the vinegar mixture, the cooked vegetables, and the chopped celery in a wide-mouthed glass or other non-reactive jar or container with a tight-fitting lid. (Don't pour boiling hot liquid into a glass container, or it may break!) Close the lid and give it a good shake. Let marinate in the refrigerator overnight before eating.

To pack into a bento, take the vegetables out of the jar with a slotted spoon or chopsticks, so that the marinating liquid is drained off. Add some store-bought cornichons or sour pickles for more variety and texture.

The marinating liquid can be reused one more time—just bring it to a boil again, let it cool, and add some freshly prepared vegetables.

AHEAD-OF-TIME NOTE: *This keeps in the refrigerator for a week. Keep well covered between uses.*

TIMELINE
The dishes in this bento should be made in advance, so there is no timeline. Simply pack and go.

VARIATION RECIPES
Portable Pies

Pies may seem like a lot of work, but I think they're worth it. Nothing is as comforting as a homemade savory pie for lunch.

Cornish Pasties

MAKES 4 LARGE PIES

I will always have a soft spot in my heart for the Cornish pasty (pronounced PAH-stee), the sturdy English turnover that miners in Cornwall carried with them for lunch. This was one of the first things that my mother bought at a bake shop in London when we moved there when I was a child.

The flaky pastry is traditional, but you can use Herbed Whole Wheat Crust pastry dough (see page 107) instead. I think that Cornish pasties taste better when they are on the large side, so I recommend dividing the dough into 4 pieces and making 4 large pies. When I grab a pasty with both hands and sink my teeth in, I'm my wide-eyed five-year-old self again.

For the flaky pastry crust (make a day or two in advance)	For the filling
8 oz (225g) all-purpose flour	8 oz (225g) ground beef
2 oz (60g) lard	1 small or ¼ large turnip, peeled and cut into ¼ inch (0.5cm) dice
2 oz (60g) butter (alternatively use all lard, all vegetable shortening, or all butter)	1 small carrot, peeled and cut into ¼ inch (0.5cm) dice
¾–1 cup (180–240ml) cold water	1 medium potato, peeled and cut into ¼ inch (0.5cm) dice
	1 medium onion, finely chopped
	½ tsp salt
	black pepper, to taste
	1 egg, beaten

To mix in a food processor, put the flour and fat into the food processor bowl and process using the chopping blade until the mixture is crumbly in texture. Add the cold water to the bowl a little at a time, pulsing to combine after each addition, until the mixture forms a very rough ball. The amount of cold water needed may vary from ¾ to 1 cup (180–240ml), depending on how humid your kitchen is on the day. Turn the dough onto a clean work surface and form into a smooth ball. Cover the dough ball in plastic wrap and refrigerate for at least an hour.

To hand mix, put the flour and fat into a bowl and rub together with your fingers until the fat is totally incorporated into the flour and the mixture is crumbly. Add the cold water a little at a time, mixing with a spatula, until the mixture forms a very rough ball. The amount of cold water needed may vary from ¾ to 1 cup (180–240ml), depending on how humid your kitchen is on the day. Turn the dough onto a clean work surface and form into a smooth ball. Cover the dough ball in plastic wrap and refrigerate for at least an hour.

To form the pasties, remove the dough from the refrigerator and roll out to ½ inch (1cm) thickness on a floured surface. Fold the pastry in half, then fold over again. Roll out the dough again to ½ inch (1cm) thickness, then fold over twice again. Wrap up in plastic and return to the refrigerator.

Meanwhile, mix all the filling ingredients together.

Preheat the oven to 350°F (175°C). Divide the refrigerated dough into quarters, and form each piece into a ball. Roll out each ball into a 10 inch (25cm) diameter circle. Brush the edges of each circle with water. Spoon ¼ of the filling into the middle of each circle, fold the pastry over the filling, and crimp the edges shut with the tines of a fork. Poke a few holes with the fork on the surface of the pastry. Place on a silicone baking sheet or a baking sheet lined with kitchen parchment paper, and brush the tops with the beaten egg. Bake for 50–60 minutes, until the dough is golden brown and puffy. Let cool on a baking rack.

Individual Salmon en Croute

MAKES **4** PASTRIES

Cold, pastry-encased pâtés and pies ("en croute" just means wrapped in pastry) are common dinner-party fare in Europe, where they are often to be found in delis and groceries. This simple homemade version, using store-bought puff-pastry dough, can be used for a special bento or picnic.

4 pieces of boneless, skinless salmon, 3 oz (90g) each	1 sheet ready-made puff pastry dough made with real butter
salt and pepper, to taste	
4 Tbsp sour cream or crème fraîche	3 Tbsp Dijon-style mustard
2 Tbsp chopped fresh tarragon	1 egg, beaten

Preheat the oven to 350°F (175°C).

Carefully check your salmon pieces to make sure they don't have any bones. They should all be about the same size and thickness to ensure they cook at the same rate. Season lightly with salt and pepper.

Mix the sour cream with the tarragon.

Roll out the puff pastry sheet and cut into 4 pieces. (You can reserve a little of the pastry to cut out into shapes to decorate the pastries.) Spread the mustard in the middle of each pastry piece, to about the same size as the salmon piece that will go on top. Spread half the sour cream and tarragon mixture on top of the mustard. Place a salmon piece on top of the mustard and cream. Spread the rest of the cream on top of the salmon.

Fold the pastry over the salmon to form little rectangular parcels. Carefully turn the parcels over so that the folded edges are on the bottom. Prick the tops with a fork and decorate if you wish with the reserved cutout pastry scraps. Brush the tops with the beaten egg.

Place on a silicone baking sheet, or a baking sheet lined with kitchen parchment paper. Bake for 20–25 minutes, until the pastries are golden brown and puffy. Remove from the oven and leave to cool on a baking rack.

While these pastries are delicious when warm, they taste even better when cold. They also freeze well. Either freeze the unbaked pastries before they are brushed with egg, or freeze the baked and finished pastries.

Indian Tiffin–inspired Bento

A tiffin is a midday meal in India, carried in a portable, stacked container that is itself called a tiffin. This is a tiffin-inspired bento with spicy bean nuggets, a quick curry, and a version of raita, the cooling yogurt and cucumber salad. It's packed in a thermal bento to keep the warm dishes hot until lunchtime.

CONTENTS

- Coconut and Kidney Bean Nuggets
- Quick South Asian–style Chicken Curry
- Chunky Cucumber Raita
- Basic Brown Rice

Coconut and Kidney Bean Nuggets

2 SERVINGS (6 NUGGETS)

These mildly spicy little morsels are great on their own or dipped into the raita.

15 oz (425g) can kidney beans, well drained
2 Tbsp desiccated coconut flakes
¼ tsp ground cardamom
1 tsp peeled and finely chopped fresh ginger
2 Tbsp fresh bread crumbs
¼ tsp ground cumin
1 tsp finely grated lemon peel
¼ tsp red chili powder, or to taste
½ tsp salt
¼ tsp black pepper
¼ cup (15g) roughly chopped fresh coriander leaves
vegetable oil, for frying
lettuce to line the container

Put all the ingredients, except the vegetable oil and the lettuce, in a food processor and process until combined. Form into little round flat patties, and refrigerate for at least an hour or overnight.

In a frying pan, heat ½ inch (1cm) of vegetable oil over high heat until the oil is smoking slightly. Lower the heat to medium. Fry the nuggets for about 4–5 minutes on each side until browned and crispy. Drain well on paper towels and let cool before arranging on a bed of lettuce.

Quick South Asian–style Chicken Curry

2 SERVINGS

This is a light, South Asian–style curry made with a crushed tomato base. Purists may not like the use of ready-made curry powder, but it's quick and does a good job. This dish is a great way of using up any little bits of leftover cooked vegetables.

1 medium onion, sliced
1½ Tbsp olive oil
1 Tbsp peeled and finely chopped fresh ginger
2 garlic cloves, finely chopped
1 medium carrot, chopped into small chunks
2 Tbsp garam masala
2 Tbsp curry powder
½ Tbsp red chili powder, or to taste
1 tsp salt
15 oz (425g) can crushed tomatoes
½ cup (120ml) coconut milk
½ cup (130g) any kind precooked or frozen vegetables—green beans, peas, cauliflower, broccoli, corn, etc.
6 oz (170g) boneless, skinless chicken breast, cut into small chunks
black pepper, to taste

In a medium-sized saucepan, sauté the onion in the olive oil over high heat until the onion is limp and lightly browned. Add the ginger, garlic, and carrot. Lower the heat to medium, then add the spices and stir briefly—they will emit a wonderful fragrance into your kitchen.

Add the salt, tomatoes, and coconut milk to the pan, and bring to a boil. Lower the heat to a simmer, and cook for 15 minutes. Put in the vegetables and bring the sauce back up to a boil. Add the chicken and simmer until the chicken is just cooked through—this should only take 3–4 minutes. Add the black pepper. Taste and adjust the seasoning if needed.

AHEAD-OF-TIME NOTE: *This tastes even better if made the day before and reheated.*

Chunky Cucumber Raita

3–4 SERVINGS

Raita is a classic Indian condiment that makes a cooling accompaniment to spicy dishes. I've added a lot more cucumber than usual here to make it a salad rather than a dip.

3 inch (8cm) length English cucumber, thinly sliced
½ tsp salt
1 cup (200g) Greek yogurt
1 tsp chopped fresh mint leaves
½ tsp ground cumin

Sprinkle the cucumber slices with the salt, massage with your hands to rub the salt in, then squeeze to expel excess moisture.

Mix the rest of the ingredients together in a bowl and add the cucumber.

This can be eaten immediately or made the night before.

Basic Brown Rice

1 SERVING

This bento is made with 1 cup (200g) hot cooked Basic Brown Rice (see page 53).

Either set the timer on your rice cooker the night before so that the rice is ready in the morning or defrost some precooked frozen rice in the microwave (see page 118). See page 16 for how to make great-tasting bento rice.

Pack hot rice from the rice cooker or microwave directly into one of the insulated containers.

TO PACK THIS BENTO IN A THERMAL LUNCH JAR

In Mumbai, a tiffin is brought to you hot from home by a delivery person called a dabbawalla. For those of us who don't have access to the services of a dabbawalla, a thermal lunch jar is ideal for this bento. Pack the rice in one of the insulated containers, and the curry in another. Put the kidney bean nuggets in one of the non-insulated upper or side containers, since they don't need to be kept warm (and if they are, they may turn a bit soggy). See Bento Boxes and Accessories (page 114) for more about thermal lunch jars and how they work.

The raita can be packed in another non-insulated side container of the thermal lunch jar set, but if you prefer it to be cool at lunchtime, pack it in a container that is separate from your thermal lunch jar, together with an ice pack.

TIMELINE

MINUTES	10	5	0
Curry	☑ reheat curry until piping hot	☑ put curry into insulated container	
Nuggets, rice (precooked), and raita	☑ pack raita into non-insulated container	☑ pack nuggets into container with lettuce ☑ pack rice into insulated container	
Thermal lunch jar prep and packing	☑ boil water in electric kettle or on stovetop ☑ pour boiling water into outer container, leave for 2 minutes	☑ pour out boiling water, wipe containers	☑ pack inner containers into outer container, put in insulating bag

Make in advance: Curry.
                              Nuggets.

Prep the night before: Set timer on rice cooker, if using.
Transfer frozen components to refrigerator to defrost.
Wash and dry lettuce to use as liner.
Make Raita.

Makiko's Essential Bento-making Equipment

Rice cooker with timer function

If you are making rice-based bentos regularly, a rice cooker with a timer function you can set the night before so that the rice will be ready in the morning is the best time-saver you can get. Rice cookers can be used for cooking grains other than rice, and many other foods too.

The basic rule for buying a rice cooker is to get the best one you can afford, but with just the functions you need and will use. A good rice cooker will last you for years.

One small and one large frying pan with nonstick coating

I do the majority of my bento cooking in two nonstick frying pans—a 7 inch (18cm) one, and a 12 inch (30cm) one. The small one is great for cooking single portions and for egg dishes, and the large one is handy for dishes such as stir-fries or for making batches of food to freeze. They are easy to clean, and only need a minimal amount of oil to prevent food from sticking.

Small to medium saucepans with lids

To use for boiling and poaching foods. Use pans with heavy bottoms for maximum heat efficiency, and don't use too much water if you are only cooking a small amount of food.

Electric kettle

An electric kettle boils water much faster than a kettle or pan on the stove, saving valuable minutes in the morning.

Sharp knives, peeler, vegetable slicer, and flexible cutting boards

Sharp knives are essential for any kind of cooking, but are very important for bento preparation. The knives I use the most are a regular-sized kitchen knife and a small fruit or paring knife. I also use a vegetable peeler a lot.

As for cutting boards, I am in love with the thin, flexible kind for bento work; I keep one for meat and fish, and another one for fruit and vegetables so I don't have to keep washing just one board to avoid cross-contamination—an important time-saving point. I can also lift the board up and bend it to pour right into the pan without spilling anything. The boards are inexpensive and take up minimal storage space.

A gadget that is not essential, but very handy to have, is a multi-use vegetable slicer and chopper or mandoline to quickly slice or grate foods.

Freezer bags, plastic wrap, and freezer storage containers

A "freezer stash"—small amounts of bento-friendly foods that are precooked, cooled, and frozen—help to keep my bentos varied and interesting with minimal fuss. These precooked portions need to be wrapped and packed securely before freezing, to avoid freezer burn. I usually wrap each portion in plastic wrap, then put the wrapped portions in heavy-duty freezer bags or plastic freezer containers.

Cooking chopsticks and tongs, and long handled tweezers

Long wooden or bamboo cooking chopsticks are very handy for stirring food during cooking, as well as for transferring food to a bento box and arranging it. Manipulating chopsticks may take a little getting used to, but it's well worth making the effort. If chopsticks are too difficult, cooking tongs work well too.

For very delicate food arranging, tweezers can be helpful. These are long handled tweezers that are meant for crafts and surgical use, not the kind you use on your eyebrows! Tweezers like these can be purchased at craft supply stores.

Decorating equipment: cookie cutters, nori punches, rice molds, small craft knives

I don't make decorations for all of my bentos, but when I do, these items are handy to have.

You can buy decorative cutters specifically meant for bento use very easily these days by mail order, but with just a little imagination, you can use things that you may already have around the house. You can find small cutters at cake-making and sugarcraft suppliers, as well as at the craft store (my favorite ones are meant for polymer clay crafts). Use straws or the narrow metal pipes used in model making to cut tiny circles out of thin slices of cheese, ham, cooked egg, or other foods. Small, sharp knives and small scissors used in needlecrafts, decoupage, and other crafts are great for cutting little pieces out of thin sheets of nori seaweed, and paper punches can be used as well. Just make sure to keep your repurposed craft supplies for food only!

Rice molds can be useful for forming onigiri rice balls. They can also be used for molding other foods, such as mini-burgers or cooked eggs.

Bento Boxes and Accessories

See page 127 for retail sources of the types of bento boxes and accessories mentioned here.

How to choose a bento box

The bento lifestyle not only makes preparing your lunch more fun, it can lead to an enjoyable and addictive hobby—collecting bento boxes and accessories.

Always select a bento box that is the appropriate size for the person eating the bento. Japanese bento boxes are sized in milliliters, and as a general rule, the size in milliliters (ml) indicates the approximate number of calories the box can hold when packed very tightly, Japanese style. For instance, a small child might require a 250ml to 350ml box; an average adult may go for a 500ml to 700ml box; and someone with a hearty appetite, such as a growing teenager or very active adult, would need a 900ml to 1100ml box or bigger.

For loosely packed bentos, such as salads, you will need a larger box. I often use a 1100ml capacity bento box for packing a salad lunch.

Bento boxes are often marked with their ml capacity, but if yours isn't, just fill it up with water to the rim and empty out that water into a measuring cup with milliliter markings to see how much it can hold.

Plastic bento box with single clip-on lid

This type of bento box has a silicone or rubberized rim to prevent liquids from leaking, and a lid with clip-on elements. It is usually single tier, although you can find two-tier boxes too. This type of box has a simpler design and fewer parts than the type of box with inner and outer lids, so it may be easier to handle for children. Boxes like these can usually be microwaved or put in the dishwasher without the lid, but first check the instructions that come with the box or ask the seller.

Plastic bento box with inner and outer lids

This is the most common type of bento box and comes in the widest variety of designs and sizes. These boxes often have both an inner flexible silicone or plastic lid that fits tightly over the container to prevent the contents from leaking, and an outer lid that is often decorated. The whole box is kept securely closed with an elastic bento band, which is usually supplied with the box. This type of box comes in one or two tiers, but two-tier models are more popular these days, because the tiers can be stacked together to take up less space when carried upright in a briefcase or bag. Two-tier boxes may have an inner leak-resistant lid for each tier. Many boxes of this type are microwave and dishwasher safe, but always check the manufacturer's or seller's instructions.

Stainless-steel box

If you want to avoid using plastic as much as possible, a stainless-steel bento box may be for you. It usually comes with a silicone sealing element around a latched lid (that can be removed for washing) to prevent leakage, but is otherwise plastic free. A stainless-steel box can be put in the dishwasher and is a pleasure to hold, but is a bit heavier than a plastic box and more expensive. This type of box comes in one and two tiers.

Aluminum box

Aluminum was the standard material for bento boxes until the early 1980s, but it's becoming rarer these days. You can still find small, colorful aluminum boxes aimed at kindergarten children (many Japanese kindergartens have special bento-box heaters, which can heat up metal boxes but not plastic ones), as well as plain ones with a retro 1960s look designed to appeal to adults nostalgic for the bento boxes of their childhood. An aluminum box is lightweight, but you should not use it for very acidic foods, which might actually corrode the aluminum if they are in prolonged contact with the surface.

Wooden bento boxes

Once, most bento boxes were made of wood. Nowadays, there are three main types of wooden bento boxes available.

A magewappa bento box is made of untreated Japanese hardwood similar to cedar. The best known magewappa boxes come from Akita Prefecture in northern Japan. A magewappa box is constructed in a manner similar to Shaker-style round wooden boxes, with the sides constructed of straight-grain wood that is bent and formed into a curved shape. The untreated wood looks and smells wonderful, and helps to keep rice tasting fresh, but can stain rather easily and needs to be handled with some care. Use inner cups for any food that could stain the wood. Hand wash the box and dry it out completely between uses by leaving in an airy location out of direct sunlight.

A coated wooden box usually has a protective, food-safe finish that brings out the natural beauty of the wood grain. It should be handled with care, but can withstand a little more handling than untreated wood or lacquerware. For instance, it can be washed with a mild dishwashing detergent. Some of my favorite bento boxes are the coated wooden type.

A natural lacquerware box is also a beautiful small work of art, and is very expensive. It also needs to be hand washed and dried out carefully with a soft cloth completely between uses, and should never be washed in dishwashing detergent.

Never put a wooden bento box in the microwave or dishwasher. Properly taken care of, a wooden bento box can become a treasured family heirloom.

Thermal lunch jars and insulating bags and boxes
A thermal lunch jar differs from a simple insulated bag or container, which merely keeps your food warm or cold for a couple of hours: it will keep your food actually hot.

A thermal lunch jar has a stainless-steel cylindrical unit that is heated up with boiling water. Insulated containers of hot food are placed in the stainless steel casing, which in turn is put into an insulated bag for carrying. Read the manufacturer's instructions carefully to see how to prepare the containers, so that your food stays as hot as you want it to. I don't use thermal lunch jars that often, since they tend to be rather bulky to carry around. It's great to be able to open up a steaming hot container of soup at lunchtime on a cold day, though, and a thermal lunch jar makes this possible. A thermal lunch jars is usually not microwave or dishwasher safe.

To simply keep your food warm or cool until lunchtime, use an insulated container or bag to carry any plastic or stainless steel bento box. (I don't recommend carrying food that's to be kept hot and cold in wooden bento boxes, since the wood may become damaged by absorbing too much moisture or odor from the food.) Make sure the food is as warm (or cool) as possible when you pack it. To keep food cold, put a small ice pack inside the insulated container or bag next to the bento box. Some bento boxes come with a handy built-in ice pack.

Boxes for onigiri rice balls and sandwiches
There are small boxes meant to carry single onigiri rice balls, as well as domed boxes where several onigiri can be held in the upper compartment, with a side dish or two packed in the lower sealed compartment.

A sandwich bento box usually has mesh sides to allow air to circulate around the bread, preventing it from getting soggy.

Side boxes
A side box is just a smaller bento box that is used in conjunction with a larger main bento box to carry fruit, a salad, and so on. Use a side box when a certain food has a distinctive flavor or a particular temperature requirement. For example, a side box is used in the Fried Shrimp Bento (page 23) to carry a salad, and in the Soboro Bento (page 43) for some fresh strawberries.

Bento-box alternatives

You don't have to buy a bento box to make bentos. An inexpensive plastic food container with a rubberized leak-resistant seal, or leakproof screw-top lid, can be used instead. Small, compact containers work well for Japanese-style bentos, while larger ones are more suitable for salad or sandwich bentos.

Lunch boxes for camping and hiking can make great bento boxes. They can be plastic or metal (usually lightweight aluminum), and are very portable.

Dividers

I like to use bento divider cups to separate flavors that shouldn't mingle. You can buy cups made of paper, aluminum foil, plastic, or silicone, but I prefer reusable silicone cupcake or muffin liners. These are dishwasher safe, really durable, and come in many shapes and colors.

The plastic grass-shaped dividers that you often see in sushi sets served at less expensive restaurants in Japan are called *baran*. Originally, baran were made of real bamboo and other leaves, and some establishments still use these natural materials. Plastic baran come in all kinds of colors and designs besides imitation grass. I don't use baran a lot in my bentos, however, since they can really only be reused a couple of times before they have to be tossed. I use salad leaves and snow peas as edible dividers instead. Baran can be a great way to add a quick splash of color to your bento box, though, as well as adding some structure and organization—rather like folders for organizing your papers neatly in a filing cabinet.

Sauce containers

For sauces, there are many different types of bottles and tiny containers available from suppliers of bento accessories. Bottles with screw-on stoppers are recommended for very liquid sauces like dressing and soy sauce, while containers with snap-on lids are suitable for mayonnaise and other thick sauces.

Picks

Bento picks are not only practical for skewering foods together and as secondary eating utensils—they come in so many fun designs that they are the easiest way to decorate your bento. Think of picks as bling for bento! Cocktail sticks and party picks can be used as well.

Utensils and wrappings

You can have as much fun with the utensils and accessories as with the bento boxes! Chopsticks and fork-and-spoon sets for bentos come in all kinds of colors and designs. I also like using a spork (one utensil that is a combination of spoon, knife and fork), available from camping suppliers.

A traditional way of wrapping a bento box is with a small-sized furoshiki, a square fabric that can be folded and knotted in various ways to form an instant carrying bag. Just place your bento box in the middle of the fabric square on the diagonal, bring two opposing corners up and above the box, and knot them. Repeat with the two other corners. You can use a large handkerchief or bandanna if you can't get hold of a bento furoshiki.

A bento box is often secured closed with an elastic band called a bento belt. If you're crafty you can make your own with wide elastic and fabric.

Weekly Meal Planner with Bento Lunch

This is a form that I designed for planning out a week's worth of meals, including a daily lunchtime bento. The bento lunch part of the planner is divided up like a mini–bento box into sections that are labeled *protein*, *carb*, *veg*, and *fruits/snacks*, to help you remember to maintain a good balance of various foods. The form includes space for a shopping list and other notes.

You can download a free printable PDF version of this form from the Just Bento web site at the following address:

http://justbento.com/weekly-meal-planner-with-bento-lunch

A simpler form just for planning out your bentos is also available:

http://justbento.com/handbook/downloads/weekly-bento-planner

Both forms are available in English, Spanish, French, German, and many other languages — even Japanese!

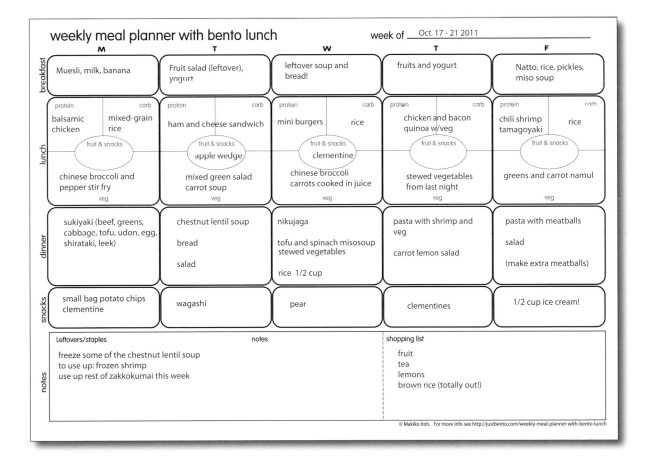

Bento Staples

There are a few foods that I make over and over again for bentos. Many of them can be made in advance and stocked in the refrigerator, freezer, or pantry. Having these staples ready to go really speeds up my bento making.

Refrigerator and Freezer Staples

Frozen Precooked Rice

Freshly cooked rice tastes best, but having a stash of ready-to-use frozen rice is a great bento time-saver.

Cook the rice following the instructions on page 53.

Measure freshly cooked, still-warm white or brown rice into portions. I use a baking-cup measure for this, and make 1-cup (200g) and ½-cup (100g) portions. Wrap each rice portion individually in microwave-safe plastic wrap while the rice is still warm. The moisture from the condensation that will be produced helps to keep the rice from drying out. Flatten the rice packets a bit with your palm, but don't crush the rice.

Place the rice packets in a single layer on a tray, ideally a metal baking sheet that fits in your freezer. When the rice packets are frozen, pack into freezer-safe bags or containers.

The rice will taste best if freshly defrosted in the morning. To defrost, use the high setting on your microwave (not the defrost setting). A 1-cup (200g) packet takes 3–4 minutes, and a ½-cup (100g) packet takes 2–3 minutes. Use up frozen rice within a month.

Refrigerator or Freezer Dashi Stock

Dashi—Japanese stock—is the base of many Japanese savory dishes. While you can make dashi using store-bought dashi granules, homemade dashi tastes so much better. The traditional way of making dashi is to simmer konbu seaweed, bonito flakes, or small dried fish called *niboshi*, in water. This method of making dashi in the refrigerator is even easier. I usually have a large, closed jug of this ready to go.

8-inch (20cm) length konbu seaweed
large handful bonito flakes

Fill a plastic or glass container that has a tight-fitting lid with water. Add the konbu seaweed and the bonito flakes. Leave in the refrigerator for at least several hours or overnight. Strain out the bonito flakes before using.

This refrigerator dashi keeps for about a week. To store it longer, pour the strained dashi into ice-cube trays and freeze. Frozen dashi will keep for up to 3 months.

Presoaked Dried Shiitake Mushrooms

I use dried shiitake mushrooms so much that I usually have a closed jar of a few of them soaking in water and ready to go in the refrigerator. Simply put a few whole dried shiitake mushrooms in a jar or other container with a tight-fitting lid, and cover with cold water. They will be soft enough to use in an hour and will keep for about a week in the refrigerator. The water can be used as a soup stock. The stems will soften enough to chop up finely and use in soups, stir-fries, and many other dishes.

Frozen Grated or Chopped Ginger

Ginger is called for in so many recipes that it's really handy to have ready to go. I periodically grate or chop up a quantity of fresh peeled ginger root and freeze it.

To freeze grated ginger, I grate it with a fine-toothed grater and put it into a plastic ziplock bag and press it flat, so that it freezes into a sheet. Whenever I need some grated ginger, I just break off a small piece of the ginger sheet.

To freeze chopped ginger, I first use a food processor to chop up a quantity, then store it loosely in a plastic ziplock bag. Take out a bit whenever a recipe calls for chopped ginger.

Frozen ginger keeps in the freezer for a month.

STORE-BOUGHT FREEZER ITEMS TO STOCK

Frozen peas
Frozen edamame beans, both in the shell and shelled
Frozen mixed vegetables of all kinds
Frozen uncooked shrimps, peeled or whole
Frozen berries

STORE-BOUGHT REFRIGERATOR ITEMS TO STOCK

Japanese or Western pickles and cornichons
Miso
Gari or beni shoga pickled ginger

Pantry Staples

Sushi Vinegar
MAKES 6 CUPS (1.4L)

You can buy ready-made sushi vinegar, but it's easy to make your own. Adjust the amount of sugar to suit your taste. This recipe makes 6 cups (1.4L) of sushi vinegar, which lasts for a long time, but you can halve or even quarter the quantities.

4 cups (1L) rice vinegar
7 oz (200g) sugar
6 Tbsp sea salt

Combine all the ingredients in a pan. Stir over low heat until the sugar and salt have dissolved. Let cool, and put into a clean bottle or jar. This keeps indefinitely. Sushi vinegar can be used in dressings and sauces, as well as for making sushi rice.

Sesame Salt
MAKES 3½ oz (100G)

Sesame salt, also known as *gomashio* or *gomasio*, is a versatile condiment that can be sprinkled over plain rice, vegetables and much more. Making your own is much more economical than buying it, and you can adjust the saltiness to suit your taste. This method permeates each sesame seed with salt—delicious!

⅓ oz (10g) salt
½ cup (120ml) water
3½ oz (100g) black or white raw sesame seeds

Dissolve the salt in the water. Put the sesame seeds and salted water in a large, nonstick frying pan over medium-low heat, stirring often with a wooden or nonstick spatula, until the moisture has completely evaporated. If the salt adheres to the pan, scrape it off with the spatula. Remove the sesame seeds from the pan once they start to pop and jump. Let cool completely, then pack into an airtight container and store in a cool, dark place. Sesame salt lasts for up to 6 months.

Garlic-infused Olive Oil

This flavorful olive oil can be used as a base for dressings as well as for sautéing anything that calls for some garlic flavor.

Put some fresh olive oil into a bottle or jar, leaving a little space at the top. The olive oil doesn't have to be the best, extra virgin kind. Fill up the bottle or jar with several peeled garlic cloves until the container is full. The more you put in, the stronger the flavor of the oil will be.

Leave the oil on your kitchen counter, where you will see it daily. Give it a good shake at least once a day. It's ready to use after a week. After a month, strain out the garlic. You can put in a sprig of rosemary and another clove of garlic for decorative purposes if you like. Rosemary gives the oil a Mediterranean scent. Alternatively, add a couple of dried hot red chili peppers to give the oil some heat.

STORE-BOUGHT PANTRY ITEMS TO STOCK

Japanese Ingredients

Dark Japanese soy sauce	White and black sesame seeds
White or mild miso (refrigerate after opening)	White and brown rice
Hon-mirin	Bonito flakes
Saké	Dried shiitake mushrooms
Rice vinegar	Shichimi pepper
Nori seaweed	Sansho pepper
Other dried seaweed: hijiki, wakame, and konbu	Dashi granules
	Sesame oil

Not-so-Japanese Ingredients

Salt, black pepper	Dijon-style mustard
Spices such as nutmeg, cinnamon, cumin, coriander, nigella seeds, mustard seeds, garam masala mix, turmeric, hot chili, paprika, cardamom seeds	Dry mustard powder
	Olive oil
	Canola or peanut oil for frying
	chili oil
Dried herbs: thyme, rosemary, oregano, herbes de Provence	White wine, red wine, and balsamic vinegar
All-purpose white flour	Hot chili sauces and pastes such as sriracha and harissa
Cornstarch	Canned beans: kidney beans or chickpeas, white navy beans, or cannellini beans
White and brown sugar	Dried pasta and noodles
Ketchup	Various grains—quinoa, barley, millet
Worcestershire sauce	

I also have a selection of fresh herbs growing in pots in the warmer months: shiso, basil, mint, parsley, coriander, chervil, and chives are my favorites for cooking.

Glossary of Japanese Ingredients

abura-age
Thinly sliced, golden brown rectangular sheets made from tofu that is deep-fried using a special process that causes an air pocket to form inside. The air pocket is often stuffed with rice (such as for Inari-zushi, page 69), vegetables, and other fillings. Abura-age can also be chopped into small pieces and used in soups and simmered dishes. Available in the refrigerated section of a Japanese grocery store, next to the tofu.

bamboo shoot
The young shoot of the bamboo plant. Bamboo shoot has a crunchy texture and a fairly neutral taste. Fresh bamboo shoot (which is hard to obtain outside of Japan) is only available in the early spring, but canned and vacuum-packed precooked bamboo shoot is available year round.

beni shoga. *See* **ginger, pickled**

bonito flakes
Shavings or flakes of dried bonito fish, known as *katsuo-bushi* in Japanese, are a main ingredient of dashi stock, and are also used as a condiment sprinkled onto vegetables or tofu, as a rice-ball filling, and more. Bonito flakes are a staple item in most Japanese kitchens.

burdock root
This long, fibrous root, known as *gobo* in Japanese, is used in dishes such as stir-fries, stews, and soups. Spicy stir-fried burdock root, called Kinpira Gobo (page 57), is a very popular vegetable dish for bentos. Soak burdock root in cold water for 15 minutes before using to get rid of the slightly muddy flavor.

daikon radish
A large, long or round white root vegetable. Raw daikon has a crunchy, peppery flavor, but when cooked it turns soft and rather sweet. Winter daikon is sweeter than summer daikon. Daikon radish can be used in stir-fries, soups, salads, and for quick pickles. Grated raw daikon is used as a refreshing condiment to accompany meat, fish, and tofu dishes. The peppery sprouted seeds of daikon radish are used in salads and as a garnish.

dashi
Dashi is the soup stock that forms the basis of many traditional Japanese dishes. It is usually made from an infusion of, or by simmering, one or more of the following ingredients: konbu seaweed, bonito flakes, small dried fish (niboshi), or dried shiitake mushrooms.

Instant dashi granules can be a handy ingredient to have in the kitchen. Some instant dashi contains monosodium glutamate (MSG), but there are now several MSG-free brands available, labeled "natural," "no additives," or *mutenka* (the Japanese term for "no additives," written 無添加 in Japanese). Look for them at Japanese groceries. Also available are dashi bags, tea-bag-like packs that can be thrown into a pan of water to make dashi instantly.

edamame
Green, immature soybeans. Both shelled and unshelled frozen edamame are increasingly available in regular supermarkets in the US, as well as in Asian or Japanese grocery stores. Edamame are highly nutritious and easy to incorporate into your bento, so I like to keep a bag or two stocked in the freezer at all times.

enoki mushrooms
Pale mushrooms with long, thin stems and small white caps. Used mostly for their crunchy, chewy texture. Also known as straw mushrooms.

furikake
A fine dry or semi-dry savory condiment that is sprinkled onto rice, salads, and other foods. Commercial furikake usually contains toasted sesame seeds, bonito flakes, and shredded nori seaweed. Available at any Japanese grocery store, furikake is very popular for bentos, since it perks up plain rice instantly.

gari. *See* **ginger, pickled**

ginger, fresh
Fresh root ginger is used extensively in Japanese cuisine. It is peeled and grated and added to meat dishes, chopped fine and added to stir-fries, and more. Keep ginger wrapped in a piece of paper towel in the refrigerator, or grate up a quantity and freeze (see page 118).

ginger, pickled
Japanese pickled ginger comes in two main varieties: *beni shoga*, which is rather salty and is usually dyed red or dark pink and shredded finely; and *gari*, which is sweeter, sliced thinly, and pale pink in color. *Gari* is used mostly as a garnish for sushi, and *beni shoga* is used in dishes such as noodles or savory pancakes.

hatcho miso
A premium miso made in Japan's Tokai region (the three prefectures of Aichi, Mie, and Gifu in present-day

Japan). In feudal times it was so highly regarded that it was served to the emperor. It is made of soybeans only, without the usual addition of rice, barley, or other grains. It is of medium sweetness and saltiness, and is a good general-purpose miso. *See also* **miso**

hijiki seaweed
Sold in the form of thin dried black strands, hijiki is very high in fiber and minerals. To prepare for cooking, rinse in cold water and leave to soak in enough water to cover until the strands become plump and soft. Drain away the soaking water before cooking.

hon-mirin. *See* mirin

kabocha squash
A winter squash with sweet, dense flesh and dark green or bright orange skin. A whole kabocha is about 8–10 inches (20–25cm) in diameter, and should feel very heavy. Kabocha is increasingly available at farmers' markets and grocery stores in North America and Europe. Common varieties are Delica, with dark green skin and orange or yellow flesh, and Hokkaido Kuri, an onion shaped variety with orange skin and lighter orange flesh. Kabocha squash is also known as Japanese pumpkin.

konbu seaweed
This thick, dark, leathery seaweed with a fine white powdery coating is a main ingredient of dashi stock. It is also eaten for its own sake—stewed, marinated, pickled, or roasted.

lotus root
The rhizome of the lotus plant, called *renkon* in Japanese. Lotus root has a crunchy texture and a pretty, lacy appearance. It is usually stewed, or blanched in vinegared water (which prevents it from discoloring) before using in salads and sushi. Available fresh and vacuum-packed, parboiled, or frozen in Asian grocery stores.

maitake mushrooms
Brown, frilly mushrooms that grow in clusters. Also known as hen-of-the-woods, these mushrooms are prized for their distinctive texture and fragrance. In Japanese cooking they are used in tempura, stir-fries, and stews. Don't let them soak in water; simply wipe off any dirt with a damp paper towel or cloth and tear apart the clusters.

mirin
This sweet fortified liquor made from rice, used exclusively as a cooking ingredient, not as a beverage, is a key ingredient in Japanese cuisine. It is used in many savory dishes to add an underlying sweetness and depth. Hon-mirin is naturally made mirin with an alcohol content of about 15–20 percent, while aji-mirin (often labeled as "cooking mirin") is an almost alcohol-free mirin-flavored condiment, and often contains additives such as salt, sugar, and MSG. A decent substitute for mirin is sweet sherry.

miso
Salty soybean paste, often with ingredients such as rice, wheat and barley mixed in, that is fermented for a year or more until it develops a deep, almost meaty flavor. Miso comes in many varieties and levels of saltiness, and is used in a wide variety of dishes. Red and white miso are the two most common types. Red miso has the stronger flavor. For general cooking purposes, white (actually light brown) miso is the most versatile, and is the type used in most of the recipes in this book. Store miso in an airtight container in the refrigerator. *See also* **hatcho miso**, **moromi miso**

mitsuba
A green leafy herb that is used as a garnish in soups and other dishes.

mizuna
A green leafy vegetable with white, crispy stems and feathery leaves. Mizuna is delicious raw in salads, quickly blanched, or in soups. Available on its own or in mesclun salad mixes.

moromi miso
A mild, chunky miso made only from soybeans, salt, and flavoring. It is usually used as a condiment, not in cooking, since subjecting it to heat adversely affects its unique texture and delicate flavor. *See also* **miso**

myoga
The tender flower buds of a type of ginger plant (*Zingiber mioga*), which taste like a cross between fresh ginger and shallot. Most often used finely sliced as a condiment with cold noodles, tofu, and other dishes, especially in the summer. You can sometimes find myoga at large Japanese grocery stores.

nerigoma. *See* sesame paste

nori seaweed
A dried seaweed, dark green to green-black in color, that comes in shiny, paper-thin dried sheets. It is used as a wrapping for rice dishes such as onigiri rice balls, grilled rice cakes, and sushi rolls. It is also shredded and used as a topping for various dishes, or cut into shapes and used to decorate food. Keep nori sheets in an airtight container in a cool, dry location. To revive slightly stale nori, hold a sheet for a few seconds on each side several inches above a stovetop burner flame, being careful not to burn it. Alternatively, put several sheets of nori on a baking sheet and dry in the oven at 300°F (150°C) for a couple of minutes.

Standard nori sheets are approximately 7 x 8 inches (18 x 20cm) in size. You can also find precut nori, as well as nori flavored with various salty ingredients.

panko
Panko are large and jagged dried bread crumbs. They are ideal for deep-frying as they don't absorb much oil and maintain a very crunchy, crispy texture. The word itself just means "bread crumbs" in Japanese, but in the West it has come to mean this specific type of bread crumb. Panko are available at many regular supermarkets in the US, as well as in Asian grocery stores.

rice
The most common type of rice in Japan and the type of rice used in this book, is called *uruchi-mai*. In English this is called Japanese rice, Japonica rice, sushi rice, or medium-grain rice. It is most commonly available as refined, polished white rice that must be rinsed several times before cooking. Unpolished brown *uruchi-mai* rice, known as *genmai* in Japanese, is also available. *Uruchi-mai* is well suited to bentos, since it doesn't get dry and hard as quickly as other rices when cold.

It is very important to properly rinse and prepare rice for steaming to achieve an authentic flavor. See page 53 for the how-to.

While Japanese rice is becoming increasingly available around the world, if you can't get hold of it, here are some acceptable substitutes. All of these rice types should be well rinsed before cooking.

- Italian medium-grain rice varieties such as Vialone, Arborio, and Carnaroli.
- Pudding rice, available in the UK, can be used in a pinch, though it is my least favorite substitute since the grains tend to disintegrate very easily while rinsing.

Rice types that are not good substitutes for Japanese rice include basmati, jasmine, wild, or any long-grain rice. If using in bentos, these rice types need to be stir-fried or otherwise cooked with oil or butter to prevent the grains from getting dry and hard.

rice vinegar
Rice vinegar is mild and suitable for use in many recipes, such as salad dressings, sauces, and marinades. Sushi vinegar is rice vinegar with added sugar and salt (see page 119). If you can't find rice vinegar, use white wine vinegar. Balsamic vinegar can be substituted when a full-bodied, sweet flavor is required.

saké
An alcoholic beverage made from fermented rice, this is one of the national drinks of Japan. Saké is a key ingredient in Japanese cuisine, especially to play down the "gamey" flavor of fish and meat dishes. Cooking saké is sold in supermarkets but often contains additives such as salt and MSG, so I stay away from it and use regular saké instead—any decent drinking saké can be used in cooking. Dry sherry can be substituted if you can't find saké.

sansho pepper
A mildly peppery spice related to Szechuan pepper, most commonly available in ground form. It is usually used as a condiment sprinkled onto finished food rather than during the cooking process, since the flavors dissipate quickly in heat. The spring leaves of the sansho tree (called *kinome* in Japanese) are used in Japan as a garnish for sushi, soups, and various vegetable side dishes.

sesame oil
Sesame oil is pressed from toasted sesame seeds, which gives the oil a deep, rich flavor. It is mainly used as a condiment in sauces and dressings, as well as to flavor meat dishes, but it can be used in conjunction with other oils for cooking too. Add a few drops of sesame oil to regular vegetable oil when stir-frying vegetables to impart that great toasty flavor. Sesame oil can turn rancid rather quickly, so buy it in small bottles unless you use it a lot.

sesame paste
A paste made of ground sesame seeds, used in both sweet and savory dishes. Japanese sesame paste, called *nerigoma* in Japanese, is made from toasted seeds and has a thicker texture and more assertive flavor than the Middle Eastern tahini, which has a runny, oily consistency. Since Japanese sesame paste can be rather hard to get outside of Japan, tahini can be used in any recipe that calls for sesame paste, but you may want to add texture and flavor by adding some toasted whole sesame seeds.

sesame salt
Sesame salt, known as *gomashio* in Japanese, is a condiment made of black or white (actually light brown) sesame seeds and salt. Like furikake, it can be sprinkled onto rice, salads, and other foods. See page 119 for a homemade recipe.

sesame seeds
Used in a variety of ways in Japanese cooking—toasted whole, lightly crushed, ground to a powder, or turned into a paste. Both black and white (actually light brown) types are used. I keep raw sesame seeds in the freezer to prevent them from turning rancid, and toast them lightly in a dry frying pan whenever I need them. Raw sesame seeds are available at natural food stores. (Raw sesame seeds are flat, while toasted sesame seeds are rounded).

shichimi pepper
A spicy, slightly crunchy Japanese condiment that is

made up of seven ingredients, including hot ground chili pepper. The other ingredients most often used are black and white sesame seeds, dried ground orange peel, aonori seaweed, crushed hemp seed, and ground sansho pepper. It is often sprinkled on noodles and soups.

shiitake mushrooms
Available fresh or dried. Dried shiitake can be used to make dashi stock, as well as in stir-fries and many other dishes. They have a denser texture and more intense flavor than fresh shiitake. I use dried shiitake so much that I usually keep a jar of them in the refrigerator, covered in water and reconstituted, ready to use (see Bento Staples, page 118). Fresh shiitake mushrooms are delicious grilled, stir-fried, stuffed, and roasted. Store fresh shiitake mushrooms in the refrigerator, loosely packed in a paper bag or wrapped in newspaper to allow them to breathe.

shiso
The shiso leaf (often called by its botanical name, *Perilla*, in the West) has a fresh, rather minty flavor, and is great used as a wrapper around rice or other food, as well as an edible divider in bento boxes. The green-leafed variety is more versatile than the red-leafed kind, which has a bitter flavor unless it is salted. The leaves are not the only part of the shiso plant that are edible—the flower buds and the seed pods can be pickled, and the seedlings are used as a delicate garnish.

soba noodles
Thin noodles made from buckwheat flour. The dried form is widely available and convenient to use, though you can buy fresh soba noodles from specialist stores. Can be eaten hot or cold.

somen noodles
Thin wheat noodles that cook in a few minutes. Can be bought dried from Japanese grocery stores.

soy sauce
A foundation ingredient of Japanese cuisine. Soy sauce, called *shoyu* in Japanese, comes in several varieties, but the most commonly used type in Japanese cooking, and the type used throughout this book, is dark soy sauce, known as *koikuchi* in Japanese. Another type that is used in the Kyoto and Osaka region of Japan is light soy sauce, called *usukuchi*, which is lighter in color, but saltier. A third type is tamari, a thick, almost viscous soy sauce that is mostly used as a dipping sauce. Reduced-salt soy sauce is also available. Try to use Japanese soy sauce for Japanese recipes rather than Chinese soy sauce—it does make a difference in flavor.

sweet potato
The Japanese sweet potato has a reddish pink skin and white flesh. It is denser, sweeter, and more floury than the orange-fleshed variety common in the United States. You can buy the Japanese type of sweet potato in Asian or Indian grocery stores. In Japan the sweet potato is used in savory dishes (deep-fried, stewed, in soups) as well as in sweets such as dumplings.

tofu
Two main types of tofu are used in Japanese cooking: soft silken (*kinugoshi*) tofu, and firm or cotton (*momen*) tofu. Of the two, firm tofu is better suited for bento recipes, since it contains less water. Tofu used in bentos must be cooked through thoroughly, since uncooked tofu can spoil quickly. To store fresh, uncooked tofu, immerse completely in water and refrigerate. Replace the water at least once a day. Tofu that smells sour or "off" should be discarded.

turnip
The Japanese turnip is white and about the size of an extra-large chicken egg. It usually comes with the greens attached, which are delicious and high in vitamins. A fresh turnip should be very firm to the touch. Rutabaga, kohlrabi, and the Western turnip or swede can be used instead of the Japanese turnip in many recipes.

udon noodles
Thick wheat noodles. Can be bought dried from Japanese grocery stores.

umeboshi
This preserved plum is very salty and sour, and is an acquired taste for most people, though many become rather addicted to it. It has antimicrobial qualities so is often put into a bento, in the middle of a bed of rice, to keep the rice fresher for longer. Umeboshi is a popular filling for onigiri rice balls. Eat it in tiny nibbles with plain rice, especially if you are unfamiliar with it.

wakame seaweed
A dark green, semitransparent seaweed that is used in soups, salads, and vinegared dishes. Usually available dried; also available preserved in salt. The dried type is easier to handle and store. Soak dried wakame seaweed for a few minutes in cold water before using. Do not soak for too long, or it will become slimy.

yuzu
A round, slightly bumpy citrus fruit that has a fresh, sharp flavor and fragrance. Usually about twice the size of a golf ball, it is sold either unripe and bright green, or ripe and yellow-orange. Both the juice and the peel are used. The peel is available dried and ground, or mixed with sansho pepper into a paste. Sprinkle yuzu peel on salads, meat or fish dishes, and soups, or in dressings and sauces. The juice is added to dressings or used in sauces.

Index of Main Ingredients

Bento-related Web Sites and Resources

There are more and more bento blogs and other bento-related web sites popping up online every day. Please visit my site, JustBento.com, for an up-to-date list of recommended sites.

Online stores that sell bento boxes and accessories

Bento&Co	en.bentoandco.com
Casa Bento	www.casabento.com
All Things For Sale	www.allthingsforsale.com
I Love Obento	www.iloveobento.com
Japanistic	www.japanistic.com
J-List/JBox	www.j-list.com or www.jbox.com
Laptop Lunches	www.laptoplunches.com
Lunchbot	www.lunchbots.com
Amazon (US only)	www.amazon.com (search with the keywords "bento" or "lunchbox")

Where to buy Japanese ingredients

A constantly updated listing of Japanese grocery stores, organized by region, can be found on my web site:

http://www.justhungry.com/japanese-grocery-store-list

Mail-order sources of Japanese ingredients

UNITED STATES

Amazon	www.amazon.com (search for specific Japanese ingredients)
Japan Super	www.japansuper.com

UNITED KINGDOM AND EUROPE

Japan Centre	www.japancentre.com

Acknowledgments

First and foremost, I could not have even contemplated writing this book without the tremendous support and encouragement of the JustBento.com readers. Thank you!

My mother Michiko has always been an inspiration to me, in the kitchen and elsewhere. She helped me with this book in more ways than I can mention here.

A big merci and arigato to Thomas Bertrand of Bento&co for kindly lending us many of the bento boxes and accessories used in the photographs.

Thanks to editor Cathy Layne and everyone at Kodansha International for their hard work in making this book come to fruition.

Last but not least, Max, you are the best person in the world. Even if I don't tell you that nearly enough.

Makiko Itoh

Kodansha International would like to thank Bento&Co for kindly loaning us the following boxes and accessories:

Front cover, bento box; page 11, bento box and onigiri boxes; page 14, bento box; page 18, bento box; page 34, bento box and chopsticks; page 42, round bento box; page 46, orange bento box; page 54, bento box; page 62, pink bento box, onigiri boxes; page 66, black bento box; page 114, plastic bento box with single clip-on lid, plastic bento box with inner and outer lids, stainless-steel box; page 115, boxes for onigiri and sandwiches.

These and many other items can be purchased at en.bentoandco.com

Makiko Itoh was born in Tokyo and raised and educated in Japan, England and the United States. After years of living in New York City, she moved to Switzerland, where she found it difficult to find authentic Japanese cooking. This inspired her to go back to her roots and learn how to cook the food her mother and grandmother used to make, using the limited range of Japanese ingredients available to her. In 2003 she started a blog about Japanese cooking called Just Hungry.com, and in 2007, a companion blog about bento box lunches called Just Bento.com. *The Just Bento Cookbook* is a continuation of her passion for spreading the word about healthy Japanese home cooking around the world.

Visit the Just Bento home page: **www.justbento.com**